To Nan

Thank you so much for all your support and encouragement all these years. I'll always remeber you and Ioan and your kindness to me.

Melynda Jarratt

The New Brunswick Military Heritage Series, Volume 12

for Prince Edward Island or the Îles de la Madeleine, who went by bus and ferry. War brides going to New Brunswick disembarked at Sackville, Moncton, Miramichi, Bathurst, Campbellton, Saint John, Fredericton, McAdam, and every whistlestop in between.

Arrival at the train station marked the end of the fairy tale and the beginning of quite a different life for New Brunswick war brides. How each woman managed to make the transition from the excitement of wartime Britain and Europe to the relative peace and quiet of New Brunswick depended on any number of factors — many of which were beyond her control. But if she had a loving husband, a safe home environment, and economic stability, anything was possible. The men these women married came from all over the province and every branch of the services: army, navy, and air force. They ran the gamut from privates and corporals to captains and flying officers, and although there was definitely a preponderance of soldiers from the North Shore and Carleton and York regiments (infantry units which had long sojourns in Britain and Europe), they were drawn from nearly every outfit across the entire country: New Brunswickers signed up where they were living, and in the Depression, many men had moved to find work in Ontario or out west. When they came home from the war, many resettled in their native province and brought their brides with them.

Some servicemen had been in Britain for as long as six years, having arrived in December 1939 with the 1st Canadian Division. Others were reinforcements who served for lesser periods, at the front or behind the lines, working in the large administrative and support organization which developed in Britain, pushing a pen or driving an army tank. Many never handled a weapon; others saw plenty of action in Sicily, Italy, France, Belgium, Holland, and Germany. The experiences of combat veterans would haunt them the rest of their lives, and in some cases contributed to less-than-happy marriages.

In civilian life, the men cut through all social classes, from the rich to the poor, skilled and unskilled, educated and uneducated. They had all survived the Depression — some better than others. Many of them were fresh-faced teenagers straight out of high school when they left to fight in a European war — as had their fathers before them, who fought in the trenches of the First World War. Others were university graduates, or had put university on hold so they could go overseas. Depending on the length of their service, all of them had some kind of post-war gratuity, including a one-time cash payment, or a down payment on a house or farm through the *Veterans Land Act*. Some men took advantage of the free tuition for veterans to attend the University of New Brunswick or Mount Allison University.

More than half of the women who came to New Brunswick went to farms, many of them far from a city, village, or even a main road. Their husbands were third- and fourth-generation New Brunswickers of Irish, Acadian, Scottish, and English descent, who had been raised in family homesteads that were the anchor of their large extended families. It was not unusual for the men to have as many as ten siblings still at home. More than a fair share knew abject poverty first-hand, and plenty were illiterate, having attained only the most basic education before leaving school out of necessity in the 1930s to work on neighbouring farms, in the woods, or on fishing boats. These men had few skills other than what they learned in the army; although the majority of them were hard-working and conscientious, their opportunities for advancement were limited in post-war New Brunswick.

Many of them had been physically wounded — some so severely that they died young from their war injuries. Others suffered from post-traumatic stress disorder (PTSD), which, although it is taken seriously today, went unrecognized and untreated in the 1940s and '50s. More than one war bride's dream of happiness was shattered when it became obvious her husband was "not the same man" she had married. Excessive drinking and hanging out with "the boys" until all hours of the night led to some very serious marital problems for these young couples. Unknown numbers of war brides suffered physical, verbal, and emotional abuse that continued throughout their marriages.

The men were an ethnically diverse group: English- and French-speaking; white, Native, Black, Lebanese, and Italian. What they all had in common, apart from being New Brunswickers, were their wartime experience overseas and a foreign-born wife who was coming to a place she knew very little about. Whether they succeeded or failed as a couple had as much to do with the wife's own character and willingness to compromise as it did with her husband's upbringing, his attitude towards women, and his understanding of the sacrifices she had made for him.

Happiness and contentment are difficult to measure: a war bride's personal satisfaction with her marriage depended on a whole set of circumstances as unique as the woman herself. It seems that when faced with difficulties most women just dug in their heels and refused to give up. Traditional attitudes towards marriage and gender role expectations kept many women in relationships that might well have broken up today. It is a wonder that more wives did not turn around and go back home after their first few months in New Brunswick. Certainly, some who had the choice did so, but others only thought about it. Some were encouraged by their own mothers to do their duty — or, more bitterly, to lie in the bed they made for themselves. Many others simply had no choice: with babies, no money, and nobody to go back to, they had to stay.

All this drama did not go unnoticed by the different branches of government that had been tasked with the war bride portfolio. The DVA, DND, and Immigration Branch had been closely monitoring press coverage of war brides, and while most of the 1946 newspaper articles were favourable, with photographs of beautiful young women and their gorgeous babies smiling for the camera, every now and then a story would appear that shed a different light on the war bride experience. In November 1946, in response to publicity given in the British press to servicemen's wives who had been abandoned by their Canadian husbands, editorials lamenting the war brides' plight appeared in Canadian and British newspapers. Alarmed by the bad publicity, Veterans Affairs decided to undertake a survey with a view to countering the impression in Britain that Canadian war brides were unhappy. Five months later, on May 21, 1947, the department released the results of a cross-country survey of war brides to show how they were faring in their marriages to Canadian ex-servicemen. Interestingly, the survey focused on New Brunswick as a "typical example" of the war bride experience. It found that the majority of these marriages were "as successful as even the most optimistic could expect."

The DVA survey received prominent coverage in New Brunswick newspapers. An article in the Saint John *Telegraph-Journal*, headlined "NB Example of Wartime Marriages," quoted its very positive results: of 1,820 marriages, 1,760 wives were still in the province as of January 1947.

The article went on to say that of the sixty who had left New Brunswick, thirty-eight had moved to other parts of Canada or the United States, one had died, and twenty-one had returned overseas. Of the twenty-one who returned, six went with husbands who planned to settle down over there, one was a widow, another widow had only come to meet her husband's people, and another wife was called home because of her father's death. Only twelve war brides had left New Brunswick because they did not like it, and only two had obtained divorces.

Canadian newspapers lapped up the New Brunswick survey results, adding their own twist to give it local flavour. In an article titled "Most War Brides Happy But Girls Resent Label," *The Globe and Mail* interviewed Toronto-based Red Cross Deputy Commissioner Major-General B.W. Browne, who happily agreed with the survey results that most marriages were "clicking." Noting that the divorce rate among war brides was "negligible," the article shifted focus to the positive impact that 65,000 new citizens were going to have on the country. Ever mindful of Canada's large rural population, *The Globe* reported that 1,000 of the 1,820 New Brunswick war brides surveyed had settled on farms and were "generally happy." It even included a ringing endorsement from Mrs. Kathleen (Smith) Withers of Fairfield, NB, who said that she "planned to bring her parents and sisters here to live." The authors of that survey would be interested to know that Mrs. Withers was still alive and well, living in the family home in Fairfield on her ninety-second birthday in 2008. Although it took a few years, her parents and sister finally did come to this province and lived here the rest of their lives.

DVA appears to have chosen New Brunswick for its study because of the province's unique characteristics, which even today give it a special

Survey Shows Canadian War Brides Contented; N.B. Taken As Example

OTTAWA, May 21—(CP)—The Veterans Department reported today that a cross-Canada survey has "indicated that the overwhelming majority of overseas marriages of Canadian servicemen are as successful as even the most optimistic could expect."

The survey, conducted by the department and sponsored by the government's rehabilitation information committee, found that those they talked to among the more than 45,000 British and European brides had two main gripes:

1. Continuation of the "war brides" label long after their honeymoons and two years after the war.

2. The "heartbreak ship" type of publicity that springs up occasionally with a dissatisfied wife heads back to Britain or the continent.

The department quoted Maj.-Gen. B. W. Browne, C.B., D.S.O., M.C., assistant national commissioner of the Canadian Red Cross Society, as agreeing with their finding that the great majority of the marriages are clicking.

The department reported a "negligible" number of divorces among the 43,695 marriages in Britain and the 2,679 on the continent. In all, those couples have borne 20,812 children.

New Brunswick was selected by the department as a typical example of what has happened to the marriages. It welcomed 1,820 overseas wives and in January, 1,760 were still living there.

Booster Committee Drawn Up

AMHERST, N. S., May 21—A special booster committee has been appointed by the executive of the Amherst Board of Trade to install a greater spirit of civic pride and optimism into the citizens of the town. Members include G. L. Jollymore, E. T. Burgess, E. C. Farnell, Gordon Hart, and J. O. Rodgers.

At the same meeting Mayor N. Sanford was appointed to represent the Board of Trade and town of Amherst at the freight rate hearing to be held in Halifax, May 26, 27, and 28.

City Cadet Among NB.

In May 1947, newspapers all across Canada reported the results of a DVA survey which focused on New Brunswick as a "typical example" of what happened to war bride marriages. In its sunny predictions of marital bliss, the study concluded that the marriages were as "successful as even the most optimistic could expect." *The Moncton Daily Times*, May 22, 1947, p.3.

standing as the only official bilingual province in the country. With a population of 478,000 in 1946, New Brunswick would have made an ideal case study because its people, the land, and its history best represented the diversity of Canada as a whole. New Brunswick had a large French-speaking Catholic population in the north with a similarly large English-speaking Protestant population in the south. Its soldiers came from rural farms, lumber towns, fishing villages, and urban centres that were connected by a network of rail, roads, and waterways — from the highlands of northeastern New Brunswick to the central woodlands; from the river valleys and rolling farmland of the south to the Acadian and Fundy coasts. And with nearly 350 years of continuous European settlement, New Brunswick would also have been considered historically significant within the Canadian Confederation: Aboriginals, Acadians, white and Black Loyalists, Scots, and Irish, as well as other newcomers from Scandinavia, Europe, and even the Middle East, had settled the land, providing a perfect microcosm of the Canadian experience.

Only time could tell whether the happy picture painted by DVA's 1947 study would remain true for New Brunswick war brides. That winter of 1946-47 was one of the coldest on record, and the summer brought unrelenting heat —and mosquitoes. Many women had some serious adjustments to make, and not just with the climate. They all faced culture shock in varying respects: from learning a new language, and sometimes a new religion, to adapting to an entirely different set of social values. Wood stoves, outdoor toilets, and the absence of electricity took some getting used to by city girls who had never set foot on a farm in their lives. As they began to settle into rural villages, such as Upper Mills near St. Stephen and Lac Baker near Edmundston, or in urban settings like Fredericton and Moncton, they would have the chance to appraise the situation and decide if this was really what they wanted out of life.

It is not known how many war brides ultimately abandoned New Brunswick and returned to Britain and Europe in those early years. The Immigration Branch did not keep statistics of outward bound "war brides" per se, but the departure rate was likely in the range of five to ten percent: somewhere between ninety and a hundred and eighty women. That's a far cry from the twelve war brides reported by DVA as having left New Brunswick because they "did not like it." We know that many marriages foundered, and that women with access to resources did go back home — sometimes with husbands and sometimes without, a few of them making the trip back and forth more than once before making up their minds to settle down. It's also clear that many women would have gladly departed when their fairy tale turned into a nightmare. We know of several who left New Brunswick in 1947 and 1948 — and others who would have liked to leave, but could not because they didn't want to risk losing their children in a custody battle. Some just picked up and left without warning, however, and their children grew up overseas, never knowing their fathers in New Brunswick. These women are proof that the DVA study was somewhat premature in its sunny predictions of wedded bliss.

Yet, the vast majority of these eighteen hundred war brides were happy and content, and made loving homes for their husbands and families. In the following chapters we will meet more than sixty of these war brides and their children from all corners of the province. For the ordinary New Brunswicker living down the street from a war bride in the 1940s, '50s, or '60s, these women quickly became part of the social fabric of the province and an indistinguishable part of their communities. They represent the diversity of the Canadian war bride experience and the living legacy of New Brunswick's impact on a troubled world many years ago.

Scottish war bride Dorothy (Currie) and her husband Robert Hyslop, in a studio portrait taken during the war years. Dorothy settled in St. Stephen, where she and Robert raised six children. A community-minded person, Dorothy served for more than ten years as village councillor and was active in numerous organizations. Courtesy of Dorothy Hyslop

Chapter One

British War Brides

Over the course of the Second World War, more than a half-million Canadian servicemen, an estimated 45,000 of whom were from New Brunswick, were stationed in Great Britain. The "first flight" of the 1st Canadian Infantry Division, numbering more than 7,000 soldiers, landed at Greenock, Scotland, on December 17, 1939. Among them were nearly 1,000 New Brunswick servicemen from the Carleton and York Regiment, who had mobilized at Woodstock at the outbreak of war and were now part of the 1st Division's 3rd Infantry Brigade. They and their comrades from across Canada were destined for the military camp at Aldershot, Hampshire, in southern England. By February 1940, 23,000 Canadians were in Britain. By July 1941, several more Canadian formations had arrived, bringing with them soldiers of the North Shore (New Brunswick) Regiment and the 8th Princess Louise's (New Brunswick) Hussars from the southern part of the province. Other New Brunswick units, such as the New Brunswick Rangers, 90th Battery and 3rd Field Regiment, Royal Canadian Artillery (RCA), swelled the ranks of the Canadian army overseas. Many other New Brunswickers also arrived as members of the army's myriad other formations and units, from signallers to service corps members and foresters.

Nearly 48,000 Canadian servicemen married overseas during the Second World War: ninety-four percent of their wives were from

England, Scotland, Ireland, and Wales. That so many war brides were British should come as no surprise. Canadians were among the first overseas troops to come to the defence of Britain, they garrisoned the country's coasts for many years — the North Shore Regiment spent nearly three full years there before landing on the beaches of France in June 1944 — and they lingered long after the war, closing down establishments and getting people and things home.

Whether they were from Grand Manan Island in the south or Miscou in the north, rural Sillikers or urban Moncton, the New Brunswickers who served in Britain were, for the most part, young and single. They were a long way from home, they had money in their pockets, and there seemed little point in long-term planning, so they wasted no time in meeting British women.

When small town boys from New Brunswick arrived in Britain, they found themselves thrust into a completely different world. The countryside, the customs of British society, and the confusing web of regional accents and dialects were all new, and the onus was on them to adapt. This was not always easy. Coming from a mainly rural background where the biggest city, Saint John, had a population of just 52,000, and even Moncton (at 22,000) and Fredericton (at 10,000) were little more than towns by European standards, young New Brunswickers straight off the farm had a lot of adjusting to do. As Canadians, they considered themselves cousins to the British and, in fact, many New Brunswick servicemen had uncles and aunts — or, at the very least, distant relatives — living in England, Scotland, Wales, and Ireland. That gave them an immediate connection with the land and its people.

But that was where the similarity ended. Most young men who enlisted in New Brunswick had never been as far as Montreal, or even Halifax, so it took some getting used to the comparatively sophisticated and liberal atmosphere of Britain. Most, however, quickly found a common cause with the British: the war. They shared the hardships of wartime shortages, endured some of the bombing, which began in earnest in September 1940, and witnessed the suffering of British civilians. That first winter of 1939-40, in particular, was one of the coldest on record and the Canadians were not happy with their barracks at Aldershot, a British military station that had been established during the Crimean War. The buildings were cold and draughty, and the British people seemed distant. Coal was in short supply, and soon wooden bus seats and park benches began disappearing: the finger of blame was pointed at the Canadians, who were suspected of stealing wood to heat their barracks.

It took a while, but over time, the Canadians' attitude towards their accommodations and their British hosts changed as they got to see for themselves what ordinary people endured every day. When the German aerial assault on Britain began, in the summer of 1940, Canadians witnessed the many deaths and terrible devastation brought about by incessant bombing raids. Meeting locals and working with them in a common cause helped these young men, who were so far from home, to understand that the British were just like themselves — and the relationships soldiers formed with local women helped cement a bond that continues to this day.

The years of Canadian garrison duty in Britain were characterized by seemingly endless training schemes and long route marches that were intended to keep Canadian soldiers busy and get them into shape. But these were punctuated by frequent leave and a chance to get out of camp and see the Britain they had heard so much about. With a few days' leave, they could travel north by train to Scotland to visit the beautiful historic cities of Edinburgh and Aberdeen, or they could reconnect with long-lost relatives in villages and towns throughout the "old country" to see for themselves the places that were part of their family history. Others went to museums and art galleries, while a few took advantage of educational opportunities offered through volunteer organizations like the YMCA and Canadian Legion as well as the chaplain services of the army. Most, at one time or another — and for some as often as they could — headed for the high life of London, muted by the blackout but not dimmed for the entertainment it offered. Only the most confirmed teetotalers missed the opportunity to frequent a British pub. Located on almost every corner and with quaint names like The Merry Tadpole, pubs proved to be an attraction young soldiers couldn't resist. There were plenty of complaints and subsequent arrests by military police for drunken behaviour, which didn't exactly endear the Canadians to the locals. But most men were decent and law-abiding and were welcomed by Britons, who knew that the Canadians had come a long way across the Atlantic to defend the motherland for the second time in less than twenty-five years.

The soldiers' meandering around Britain was facilitated by plenty of cheap and clean accommodations for servicemen in overnight hostels operated by Volunteer Aid Detachments (VADs) like the YMCA, Red Cross, or Salvation Army. The Canadian High Commissioner, Vincent Massey, and his wife, the former Alice Parkin of Fredericton, were involved in the Beaver Clubs, which provided beds, meals, and reading rooms with up-to-date Canadian newspapers and magazines. Everywhere they went, soldiers mixed with the local population and, for the most part, made a good impression on the people they encountered along the way — especially the women.

The society that Canadians encountered was under enormous stress. The British introduced conscription early on, drawing men into the forces and essential war work and eventually conscripting women as well. Rationing, blackouts, and bombing were a way of life. More than sixty thousand British civilians were killed as a result of German air raids during the Second World War, and few were not touched by tragedy. Thousands of families living along German bombing routes or near industrial areas were torn from their homes during the Blitz, and the lucky ones survived to tell the tale. Others had the misfortune of being in the wrong place at the wrong time; their deaths were a constant reminder to everyone, including the Canadians stationed in Britain, of the deeply personal cost Britons were paying for this war with Germany.

English war bride Joyce (Ward) Buzzel of Saint John came from Eastbourne in Sussex. Joyce had a few close shaves in London during the Battle of Britain, in 1940, and was literally blown off her feet by a buzz bomb that hit Victoria Station in 1944. One of Joyce's neighbours in Eastbourne was killed by an air raid. "Her body was blown out of the house and landed in our garden," Joyce recalled. The force of the blast was so powerful that the woman's clothes were torn from her corpse:

"She didn't have a stitch on. It was an awful sight." But there was worse to come. Joyce's father, William, was a Great War veteran and he volunteered as an Air Raid Warden, enforcing strict blackout regulations. When Joyce announced that she was going to marry Sergeant Ward Buzzel, a Canadian soldier serving in the 5th Field Regiment, RCA, her father was not pleased. He already had another suitor in mind for his daughter — the King's caddy. "My father did not like it at all," she remembered. "He said Canada was too cold and told me 'Over my dead body will you marry a Canadian'." Unfortunately, William Ward was killed in an air raid exactly one week before Joyce got married on July 26, 1942. "They found his body in the rubble," she said sadly.

The same bombing and deprivation affected northern Britain. Scottish war bride May (Armstrong) Brockway was from Clydebank, a large burgh and important river port located nine kilometres northwest of Glasgow. Because of its strategic shipyards, and its munitions and aero-engine factories, Clydebank was subjected to intense German bombing raids on the nights of March 13 and 14, 1941. At the time, May was a twenty-one-year-old clerk working in a clothing store in Clydebank. Her story begins with a prophetic and disturbing dream that foresaw the experiences which lay ahead. In her dream, May was walking down a dusty, darkened road. On either side of the road were two burning tenement buildings, the flames licking up their high sides and casting an eerie glow onto her path. She continued walking through this unearthly landscape until she woke up, frightened. She remarked how close the dream was to reality: "There were two burning tenements on each side, and I'm walking down this road, and it was absolutely true of the night that I spent because I walked down the street with the buildings burned and bombed on each side. It was just as if my dream was a reality."

Jean (Attwood) Belding of Fredericton was fourteen years old and living with her parents in Hounslow, Middlesex, when the war broke out. Her father had served in the Bicycle Corps at Gallipoli during the First War and was too old for the military in 1939, so he continued to work for British Transport in what was deemed an essential service. Jean recalls that her father refused to build an air raid shelter in their back yard. "He said he had survived one war and was 'going to survive another'." So it was the height of irony that he was killed by a stray British anti-aircraft shell while riding his bicycle home from work one night in October 1940.

When the Second World War broke out, in September 1939, it was a given that every able-bodied man would join the war effort. Women, on the other hand, were expected to fulfill their traditional role of tending to family and keeping the home fires burning. At the beginning, the emphasis was on voluntarism, and women filled all kinds of jobs that previously had been done by men, the notion being that every job taken by a woman released a man for combat duty. This much had been done in the Great War. In 1939, however, the British government also encouraged women to join the new women's branches of the armed forces, and many thousands responded. Their importance increased by mid-1940, when it became clear that relying on women's sense of patriotism was not enough to meet the demands of a country now under threat of invasion.

Under the *Emergency Powers (Defence) Act* of 1940, every British woman between the ages of eighteen and sixty-one had to register and choose from a variety of jobs. In December 1941, the *National Service Act* made British women between the ages of nineteen and thirty-one liable to compulsory military service, thus marking the first time in British history that women were called up for service in the armed forces. Over time, the different women's branches of the armed services had varying age requirements, but, generally, women were accepted for military service if they fell between the ages of seventeen and forty-one.

In total, some 7.5 million women were mobilized for Britain's war effort, including 475,000 who served in the Auxiliary Territorial Service (ATS) of the army, the Women's Auxiliary Air Force (WAAF), and the Women's Royal Naval Service (WRNS). Nursing sisters, in particular, served in combat zones, and were often under fire in Africa, the Mediterranean, and Northwest Europe. Another 375,000 volunteered for Civil Defence in Air Raid Precautions (ARP) and the Women's Voluntary Services. Thirty-six thousand women drove ambulances and 73,000 were in the Auxiliary and National Fire Services. A further 80,000 women served in the Women's Land Army (an agricultural labour force), and hundreds of thousands worked in the armaments industry.

Many British women found themselves in the front lines of this total war. Some Navy, Army and Air Force Institutes (NAAFI) "girls" were buried in French and Belgian military cemeteries following the disastrous evacuation of the British army at Dunkirk in 1940. Others were killed at their workbenches when British factories were bombed, or died in the streets doing their duty as Air Raid Wardens.

Before female conscription became the rule in December 1941, volunteers filled the ranks of the ATS, WRNS, and WAAF, and more than one seventeen-year-old was so enamoured with the thought of military service that she quit a full-time job to join up. Seventeen-and-a-half-year-old Doris (Field) Lloyd of Halifax, Yorkshire, was looking for some excitement when she joined the WAAF in January 1940. Bored with her job as a grocery clerk, she begged her mother to sign the permission documents for the air force. Mrs. Field grudgingly went along, figuring the WAAF would never accept her daughter. But the women's services were desperate for recruits, and within weeks, Doris was at the Uxbridge training centre outside of London, learning how to march. Eight months later, on August 18, 1940, Doris was stationed at a Spitfire airbase in Kenley and found herself in the middle of one of the first bombing raids of the Battle of Britain. "I'll never forget it for the rest of my life," Doris said. "We ran to find cover. I remember looking into the sky and seeing so many bombers, the sky was black. They came in waves and the German fighters would come down low and machine-gun anyone who was running."

Twenty-year-old Delice (deWolf) Wilby of London had a job at her sister's dressmaking shop when the war broke out. She volunteered with the ATS, where she ended up working with top secret military documents in the heart of the city. Del met her husband, RCAF Gunner Thomas Wilby of Fredericton, at a dance, and he asked her to marry on the first date. Tom was of Lebanese descent and strikingly handsome. She thought he was crazy, but eleven days later they tied the knot.

The Wilbys were able to spend their leaves together, and in November

1942, Tom and Del planned a romantic getaway in York. Del was brimming with excitement at the news she was pregnant with their first child and planned to surprise Tom. But when she arrived at the train station that night, she was met by his commanding officer, who informed her that Tom had been forced to bail out of his aircraft over France and was missing in action. It took some time for the news to reach England that Tom was alive. As it turned out, he had broken his leg in the fall and had been rescued by French locals, who brought a doctor to tend his injuries. The doctor betrayed Tom to the Germans, and he was taken prisoner. When his leg was good enough to stand on, Tom was rescued by the French Resistance, who helped him make his way back to England over the Pyrenees.

By the time Tom arrived in England, Del had been discharged from the WAAF because of her pregnancy and had already left for the safety of New Brunswick. Ironically, her passage in a convoy zigzagging across the North Atlantic, during the worst phase of the German submarine assault on Allied shipping, was nearly as perilous as Tom's remarkable escape. Meantime, Tom was considered a high priority for repatriation and was sent back to Canada. He arrived just in time for the birth of their first son, in June 1943, and they spent the rest of the war safe and sound in Fredericton.

Eileen (Meaden) Mesheau of Fulham, London, was seventeen and a half when she volunteered with the ATS in September 1940. After basic training in Salisbury, she worked as dental assistant in the Dental Corps at Weymouth, but then moved into a new position as a plotter, following the movement of airplanes in the skies over Britain. By early June 1944, Eileen was working the night shift at the Portland Dockyards in Dorset. She recalled going in at 8:00 p.m. on June 5 and seeing thousands of men and trucks spread across the docks, and hundreds of assault ships and landing craft as far as the eye could see. "That night we plotted those boys all the way to France, and when our shift was over the next morning we emerged from the plotting room, and there was nothing but complete silence." No men, no trucks, no ships. They had all left for Normandy.

By December 1941, service was no longer optional and, under threat of severe repercussions, every young woman had to make a decision about what she was going to do for the war effort. (Exceptions were made for mothers with infants and children at home, and the elderly, ill, and infirm.) The push to enlist women into the armed forces was undermined by persistent and unfounded rumours that women in the services were "loose" — an accusation that led many worried parents to object to their daughters joining the armed forces. The belief was that young women would be exposed to inappropriate behaviour, mostly from their male counterparts; and there were fears, some of them grounded in truth, that innocent young women would get in "trouble" — a euphemism for unwed pregnancy.

Other parents wanted their daughters close by, so they encouraged them to sign up for munitions factories or work deemed "essential" before they could be conscripted. A father or mother's stern refusal was often enough to make a young woman choose another occupation from the options placed before her — but no matter what she did for the war effort, it couldn't completely rule out meeting men.

Eighteen-year-old Johan (Hillis) DeWitt of Glasgow, Scotland, was proof that Canadian soldiers could be encountered in the strangest places. She joined the Women's Land Army after her father protested that no daughter of his was going to join the WRNS. Her father imagined that Johan would be so busy tending to crops and animals that she'd have no time to meet men. Besides, he had plans to buy a farm after the war ended, so he wanted Johan to have some agricultural experience. Johan ended up working at the Dunira Estate in Scotland, where, among her many duties, she mucked out the cow barns. Unfortunately for Johan's father, the manor house on the estate had been turned into a hospital. One day, as she was in the barn pushing a wheelbarrow, Johan somehow tripped and ended up to her elbows in manure. As she looked up, she saw two Canadians standing there, laughing: she ended up marrying one of them, Private Luke DeWitt of Hartland, serving with the Carleton and York Regiment, who was convalescing at the Dunira Estate. Johan came to New Brunswick in 1946 and eventually settled in Burton.

Nurses were particularly vulnerable to falling in love with servicemen. Ann (Biles) Johnston of Glasgow was eighteen years old and just out of high school when the war began, and she joined the British Red Cross as a nursing sister. "There was no teenage life for us. I had a choice of the army, navy, air force, or nursing. If you couldn't decide, it was off to the munitions factory for you, so I chose nursing." Ann took her training at Mearnskirk in Renfrewshire, Scotland, and also worked part time as an ambulance driver. She met her first husband, Ralph Lawrence of Nashwaaksis, New Brunswick, when he was a patient at Mearnskirk.

Ann happened to be on duty one fateful night in May 1941 when Hitler's deputy, Rudolf Hess, parachuted from his Messerschmitt 110, landing in a farmer's field nearby. She recalled going out in the darkened night and seeing the farmer standing over the Nazi with a pitchfork. At the time, she didn't know much about Hess, other than the fact that he was German, but she found out later that he claimed to be on a mission to broker a peace deal with Britain. "That night we brought Hess to Mearnskirk with a broken ankle. He had that fixed and then was sent to a castle in Scotland where he stayed until the war ended." Hess was tried at Nuremburg and spent the rest of his life in prison. Ann never forgot her brush with history.

There were so many British war brides who served in the military, in the Women's Land Army, as nursing sisters, or in munitions factories during the Second World War that it seems that service was the rule, rather than the exception to their experience. But not everyone was old enough to join up: they had to finish their education first. Most British students finished school at age fourteen and then went out to work, typically in a job that required few or no skills. Girls of fourteen and fifteen would find "women's work" in the female sphere: in bake shops, as domestics, or in offices. By the time they were sixteen, they had to register for war work. When Jean Belding finished school at fourteen, she went to work in the office at W.H. Smith & Sons in Holborn, London. Later she went on to Sperry Gyroscope on the Great West Road in London. Sperry manufactured gyroscopes for the aviation industry so it was considered an "essential occupation," and thus Jean fulfilled her civic duties

The late Johan (Hillis) DeWitt in her Women's Land Army uniform. Johan wanted to join the air force, but her father objected, so she ended up on the Dunira Estate in Scotland, where she met Private Luke DeWitt of the Carleton and York Regiment. They lived in Burton, NB. Courtesy of the late Johan DeWitt

at the ripe age of sixteen. She was called up for the fire service but her mother didn't want her to go. "After my father's death in an air raid, my mother wanted me home at nights, so she went to the doctor and got a medical certificate to prove that I sleepwalked." Instead of fire service, Jean volunteered at the YMCA in the evenings, serving tea and coffee to British soldiers at the barracks in Hounslow.

New Brunswick servicemen met British women everywhere they went: at skating rinks and train stations, on buses and in queues, at dances and in theatres, in blackouts and on blind dates. The circumstances of meeting were often so extraordinary that some unions seem destined from the start. English war bride Nancy (King) Rioux of Plaster Rock met her husband in a movie theatre, where she was minding her own business watching a film. Ivan Rioux was a French-speaking soldier from Grand Falls, who had been in England since 1939 with the Carleton and Yorks. Britons, and Canadian soldiers too, had grown so accustomed to air raids that turned out to be false alarms that the audience kept watching the film in spite of the siren. When a bomb struck the theatre, the blast threw Nancy out of her seat and she landed in Ivan's

Ann (Biles) Johnston (circled) of Glasgow had an encounter with Hitler's deputy, Rudolf Hess, when he parachuted from his airplane near the Scottish hospital where she worked as a nurse and ambulance driver. Her first husband, Ralph Lawrence of Nashwaaksis, died twelve days after their marriage when his ship, HMCS *Athabascan*, was sunk in the English Channel. Ann came to Canada as a war widow. She fell in love with Jack Johnston, Ralph's next-door neighbour in Nashwaaksis, and they were married in 1947. Courtesy of Sandra Pond

lap. They were married in Caterham in February 1941, and Nancy was among the first war brides to come to New Brunswick, arriving in Grand Falls in 1942.

Most chance meetings between bride and groom were less dramatic. Some soldiers were actually billeted with families in densely packed neighbourhoods where young women and soldiers could not fail to meet. There are plenty of examples of romances that bloomed over the dinner table and backyard fence. But whether it was broad daylight or a blackout, in the middle of the street or in a bomb shelter, Canadians weren't shy about introducing themselves to women. English war bride

Hilda (Smith) Fyffe of Cornhill, near Sussex, New Brunswick, was out for a walk with a co-worker from the Leatherhead co-op in Bookham, in January 1940, when two Canadian soldiers approached them on the street. One of the men, Sam Fyffe, who had arrived in England with the Carleton and York Regiment in December 1939, tugged on her belt and asked what time she was off work. Hilda replied, "Six." To her surprise, the Canadian was at her doorstep at 6:00 p.m. the next day. A little chit-chat and an invitation into the house was all it took for the romance to begin, and a year and a half later, on June 1, 1941, they were married.

English war bride Doris (Field) Lloyd recalled seeing some soldiers from the Carleton and Yorks on parade in Caterham one day early in 1940, and as they passed by, there were loud whistles and shouts of "Hey baby!" "Englishmen would never do that," Doris said of the Canadians' straight-to-the-point approach to meeting women. "They were 'fresh,' but they were so different from anything we knew. With their accents and uniforms, we thought they were so romantic, and it's no wonder we fell in love with them." Doris married Sergeant Ralph Lloyd of the Carleton and York Regiment in December 1941.

Being "different" from Englishmen was one of the qualities that endeared Canadians to British women, but another was the fact that most of the available British men had been called up to serve in North Africa and the Mediterranean: for some time in Britain, the Canadians were the only young men around. They also made more money than British servicemen, their uniforms were nicer-looking, they had access to rations like cigarettes, sugar, eggs, and chocolate, which most British families couldn't get — even on the black market — and, most important, they loved to dance and have fun.

The dance hall was the most popular place for young couples to meet during the Second World War. Jitterbugging, waltzing, and smooching to Glenn Miller and Tommy Dorsey was a welcome escape from the anxieties brought on by the incessant bombing and tragedy that seemed to lurk around every corner. On the dance floor, young people could cast aside their worries, if only for a moment, and drift into another world where music, fun, and laughter reigned.

Twenty-year-old Betty (Silk) Smith of St. Stephen met her husband, Seldon, in March 1943 at a dance in her hometown of Preston, Lancashire. Betty said you could go to a dance at a different place "every night of the week" — something that must have been quite appealing to small town boys from a rural province. "Monday night there wouldn't be too many people, that would be a poor night to go. Tuesday night at one certain place, we always had a good dance there, and maybe Wednesday at another place; and then Thursday, Friday, and Saturday, it was guaranteed."

Not surprisingly, Canadians were pretty smooth on the ice, too. Mary (Ralston) MacKellar met her husband, Leading Aircraftsman (LAC) Jack Mackellar, on March 11, 1944, at the skating rink in Ayr, Scotland. Mary was twenty years old and had a day off from work at the Saxone shoe factory in Kilmarnock, where she made army boots for the war effort. She and her sister and a friend were skating when they were introduced to two Canadian airmen from New Brunswick. Jack MacKellar and Howard Campbell were childhood friends from Arthurette and were based outside of Ayr, where they were training with the British National Fire Service as members of a crash crew. Howard met Mary first and introduced her to Jack. The couple hit it off right away and were married in February 1946.

Coincidentally, Howard Campbell also brought home a war bride to Arthurette. Nineteen-year-old Betty Sheppee of Plymouth, England, was on holiday with a girlfriend in Bournemouth when the two young women met Howard Campbell and another Canadian airman, Bill Brittain, walking down the promenade. It was August 1945 and the war was over, but there were still plenty of Allied servicemen in Britain waiting their turn to be repatriated back home. The two women were supposed to meet American GIs for a date, but when the Canadians happened along the GIs were soon forgotten. Betty and Howard talked until 9.00 p.m. and would have kept talking, but Howard had to get back to barracks. They made arrangements to meet again the next day, and Betty said, "I knew I had just met the man of my dreams." They were married the following year, on April 17, 1946, in St. Augustine's Church vestry

Betty Campbell on her wedding day. When Betty arrived in Halifax, in early October 1946, she was asked where she was headed in New Brunswick. When she replied "Arthurette," the person roared, "Where the hell is Arthurette?" — a joke Betty loved to tell at war bride reunions. Courtesy of Angela Michaud in Plymouth. Howard was repatriated to Canada in July, and Betty followed shortly thereafter, arriving in Canada on the *Scythia* in September. At Halifax, there was a mix-up, and Betty had an eight-hour wait for the train to Arthurette. She was assigned a young corporal who had been confined to barracks for some misdemeanor, and his punishment was to make sure Betty got on the right train that evening. When she and the corporal went to get the tickets, he asked where she was headed. She told him "Arthurette, New Brunswick," and the corporal blurted out, "Where the hell is Arthurette?" — a joke Betty loved to tell when people asked about her arrival in Canada. Many years later, she had a sweatshirt made that said "Where the hell is Arthurette?" and wore it proudly at war bride reunions.

❦

With the falling in love now behind them, British women and their New Brunswick fiancés had to transform their relationships into marriage and everything that entailed, from the agonizingly slow bureaucratic process of getting permission from military authorities, to the actual wedding itself — if it didn't get cancelled at the last minute. Marriage brought with it an introduction to the Canadian Wives Bureau, which organized the war brides' journey to Canada on trans-Atlantic ocean liners like the *Queen Mary* and *Aquitania*. After a sometimes harrowing journey across the Atlantic, they landed at Pier 21 in Halifax and boarded a train headed to their ultimate destinations. Saying "I do" to a New Brunswick serviceman was an affair of the heart, but there had been little in the short lives of these young women to prepare them for what lay ahead. They had to travel to a strange new country, far from the familiar landscape of their homes and the comforting support of friends and family, and often with new babies in their arms. And they had to build a new life with the handsome young soldiers who were now their husbands. Most made that difficult transition very well, but it was not all smooth sailing.

Chapter Two

Marriage and Travel to Canada

It is not known when the first marriage between a New Brunswick soldier and British woman took place overseas during the Second World War, but Sergeant Glen Elliot's wedding to Catherine Robertson on Christmas Eve, 1940 — one of 1,220 marriages that year between Canadian soldiers and British brides — was among the earliest. They met on a bus in Aberdeen in August 1940, and, never one to mince words, Cathie let the Canadian soldier know exactly what was on her mind: "If you're looking for a good time, you may as well look somewhere else, because I'm not a good-time girl!" Glen was from Siddon Ridge in Victoria County and had been overseas with the Carleton and York Regiment since December 1939. He was not about to give up on this feisty Scottish lass, and four months later, they were married.

As the months passed and the number of weddings started to climb, both British and Canadian authorities raised concerns that too many marriages were being contracted in haste. Military officials had good reason to be worried. In the Canadian Wives Bureau files are pages and pages of "bigamous" marriages, and more than a few of them involved soldiers with the letter "G" in front of their military registration number: "G" meant they had signed up in Military District 7, which was New Brunswick.

The rules changed over the course of the war, but it seems from the outset that the plan was to increase the amount of paperwork involved

Rita (Scrase) Maunder (circled) with a group of war brides at the Brighton train station, March 1946. The Wives Bureau organized the transport of war brides from their homes to their final destinations in Canada. This group of wives travelled to the hostel in London, where they spent the night before their departure for Canada on board the *Aquitania*. Courtesy of Rita Maunder

in getting married and so discourage impulsive unions. As a military strategy, increased bureaucracy was an abysmal failure. The number of weddings of Canadian soldiers went up, in part because of the growing number of Canadians in Britain. And love could not be easily restrained by paperwork and military obfuscation.

At a minimum, soldiers had to fill out a "Permission to Marry" form and have it endorsed by their commanding officer. The latter did not always cooperate, no matter how much in love the couple claimed to be. Combat units, in particular, were training for a deadly business, and wives and sweethearts — especially local ones — were a major distraction for soldiers. If the potential bride and groom were under twenty-one, they also had to get written permission from their parents. This, too, was never a sure bet, especially if the mother or father in Canada had a local girl in mind, and vice versa for the parents in Britain. The bride-to-be had to get a letter of recommendation from her employer, or from her commanding officer if she was in the British military, and take a medical from a Canadian military-approved doctor to show she was free of communicable diseases, especially tuberculosis and venereal disease.

Couples also had to be interviewed by the padre of the soldier's unit, to see if they fully understood the implications of marriage. This, too, was not always an easy hurdle to clear. Father Myles Hickey, the Roman Catholic padre of the North Shore Regiment, described in his memoir, *The Scarlet Dawn* (1949), the task of sorting out the romantic entanglements of his "boys," who were falling in love all over Britain. In one letter, Father Hickey tried to discourage a marriage between a French-speaking Acadian soldier and a "Miss O'Brien" (a pseudonym) from Glasgow by describing to the would-be bride the mountains of snow and ice that would greet her every winter in New Brunswick. Then, in what Father Hickey believed would deliver a fatal blow to the relationship, he tried to dissuade her from marrying because her husband was francophone and nobody in his little village back in northern New Brunswick could speak English. But Miss O'Brien was not discouraged at all by Father Hickey and got her two cents' worth in with a curt reply to him the next day:

> Dear Father Hickey:
> Thank you for your letter. As to your first difficulty —
> I like snow, and secondly, love knows no language.
>
> Yours truly
> Mary O'Brien.

Another war bride, Rose (O'Reilley) Boulay, had better luck with Father Hickey, perhaps because she was Irish, Catholic, and English-speaking, as was her husband-to-be, Horace Boulay. Rose had left Ireland in 1938 to live with her sister in London and had planned to take a nursing

```
                                        1st. November      43.
                                                           CA/PC

The Commanding Officer.          Ref. Gnr. H. R. Grover. G.4268.
21st. Battery. R.C.A.
6th. Field Regt.
Base Post Office.
England.


Dear Sir,

        Miss Phyllis Rose Head, EJJI/77/3 of 14, St. James
Street Lewes, age 21 years.

        Has been in our employ for the past 22 months, she
held one post previously from the time of leaving school.

        I can personally recommend her as being honest,
industrious, sober, of good character repute. Thrifty and
domesticated.


                            Yours faithfully,

                                [signature]

                                MANAGER.
```

Prospective brides had to get a letter from their employer or, if they were in the military, their commanding officer attesting to their good character and domestic abilities. In this letter, Miss Phyllis Rose Head of Lewes, East Sussex, gets a glowing review from her employer. Courtesy of Russell Weller

> OVERSEAS SERVICE
>
> North Shore N B Regt
> / Cdn. Army, Eng.
> Nov. 5'
>
> Dear Miss O'Reily:
>
> I am the Chaplain of the Regt. and one of my boys Horace Bouley, spoke to me of your intention to marry. Now, Horace is a fine boy, from a fine Catholic family. I know them very well, and Horace is a good Catholic himself. I hope Horace has told you of conditions in Canada — how we live etc. then you will not be disappointed. So long as you love one another and are sincere about everything then everything will be fine. I hope you may be very happy, and you can be by deciding to be right now.
>
> Sincerely,
> Father Hickey

Father Myles Hickey's letter of advice to Rose (O'Reilly) Boulay, an Irish war bride who married Horace Boulay of Belledune. Horace and Rose took the padre's advice and were married on April 29, 1944, at St. Agnes Catholic Church in Cricklewood, London. Courtesy of Rose Boulay course, but the war intervened. She was working full-time at the Royal Ordnance Factory in Swynnerton, Staffordshire, filling shells, when she met Horace at a house party in London. Horace was a dispatch rider with the North Shore Regiment and came from a large farm family in Belledune, not far from Father Hickey's own family in Jacquet River. It seems that Rose's mother in Ireland was concerned about this young soldier from Canada and what kind of a family her daughter was marrying into. It was the padre's job to write to Rose and her mother with reassuring words about the young man and his people in New Brunswick. Horace died in 1999, but Rose still has the letter that Father Hickey wrote in 1946 with some fatherly advice for a good marriage. It obviously worked, because Rose and Horace were married for more than fifty years.

As Padre Hickey knew full well, weddings can be complicated at the best of times. But add a war, rationing, and military regulations, and what happened more often than not was the opposite of a young bride's dream. The typical white wedding dress, cake, and sit-down reception for family and friends were certainly not the norm. Strict rationing made it difficult, if not impossible, to purchase white material for a gown (unless the groom was in the air force and could pinch some parachute silk), eggs, flour, and sugar for a cake, or anything better than Spam for sandwiches and a few liquor rations shared among the drinkers at the party. More likely, the marriage was a quickly assembled affair, with a small group of family and close friends, that happened in spite of circumstances. And at a time when telephones were still a luxury, most communication within Britain was by letter or telegram, so urgent messages about changes in plans often got lost or muddled in the translation.

That's what happened to twenty-two-year-old Joan (Hawtin) LeBlanc of Moncton, whose June 10, 1944, wedding at St. John the Evangelist Church in Islington, London, had to be cancelled when the groom failed to show up. Arsene LeBlanc was with the 8th Battery of the 2nd Field Regiment, RCA. Joan was blissfully unaware that, just days before the wedding, Arsene had left an urgent telephone message with a neighbour down the street, saying that all leave was cancelled due to the invasion of France (which occurred on June 6). Perhaps it was his French accent at fault, but the message never reached the bride-to-be. On June 10, the church filled up with guests, but Arsene was nowhere to be found. "I'll never forget it," Joan recalled more than sixty years later. "I was in my white wedding dress, with my two bridesmaids and driver, and we were waiting at my parents' home for the signal to proceed to the church when it became obvious that Arsene wasn't going to show." Joan's parents were not impressed. The house was decorated and the tables laid out with food that was difficult to get at the best of times. A couple of guests muttered, "What do you expect from those Canadians?" Joan shed a few tears as friends and family tried to console her. Ever the optimist, the Catholic priest offered to marry them at the first opportunity, since the banns had already been read and the licence was still valid. There was brief excitement for a few minutes when Arsene's brother, Edgar, appeared in his Canadian uniform and everyone thought he was the groom. Joan was terribly disappointed with the way her wedding day turned out, but everyone agreed there had to be a good reason why Arsene didn't show, and they held the reception anyway.

Two weeks later, Arsene contacted Joan and told her the story: his leave on the 10th had been cancelled and his message had failed to arrive. He said he now had forty-eight hours' leave, starting on June 28, and did she still want to get married? Arrangements were quickly made, and on June 29, the guests and wedding party gathered once again at St. John the Evangelist Church. Just as the ceremony began, an air raid siren started howling. The priest asked, "Do you want to continue?" "Yes, but hurry up!" was their reply. Nothing was going to stop them from getting married this time. Just as they got to the part where the priest asked, "Do you take this man for your lawfully wedded husband?" a bomb exploded across the street from the church, causing serious damage to the building's exterior. After the dust settled, they continued with the ceremony and emerged from the church as husband and wife.

Mildred (Young) of Thornton Heath and Sergeant Major Harold Sowers of Sheffield, New Brunswick, were another couple whose wedding plans appeared to be jinxed. Harold, serving with the Carleton and

York Regiment, found himself entangled in a British railway strike on the other side of the English Channel, the day before they were supposed to get married. The wedding almost didn't happen — three times — and when it finally did, on August 4, 1946, the Saint John *Telegraph-Journal* printed a large, rather humorous article with a five-line headline that read:

> "Wedding Bells Ring Loudly Three Times Before Final Take
> Sgt. Major Harold Sowers and Bride-Elect Had Tough Time Getting Married
> Reception Before the Marriage
> The Minister's First Marriage in the Parish
> All Ended Happily"

For most war brides, the wedding — invariably memorable — was just the start of the adventure: they still had to get to Canada. The vast majority of war brides travelled to their new country without their husbands, and many arrived with only complete strangers to greet them. By that stage, at least half also had infants in their arms. Fewer expressions of hope and trust could be found in those dark days. Wives and children of Canadian servicemen overseas trickled into Canada under the auspices of the Immigration Branch of the Department of Mines and Resources, starting in 1942. Wartime travel on small troopships or in berths on general cargo vessels, zigzagging in a convoy across the Atlantic to avoid German U-boats and mines, was dangerous and uncomfortable. Only 1,687 dependents (1,109 wives and 578 children) braved the passage before August 1944, and of these, we know of only a handful who came to New Brunswick.

Everything changed, however, once the D-Day landings took place and the tide of war shifted in the Allies' favour. In August 1944, the Department of National Defence set up the Canadian Wives Bureau as a Directorate of the Adjutant General's Office at Canadian Military Headquarters. The Wives Bureau was divided into the Information and Welfare Section on Charles Street and the Civilian Repatriation Section at Sackville House in London. Over the course of the next 18 months, until it shut its doors at the end of January 1947, the Wives Bureau brought a total of 59,647 dependents to Canada (41,737 wives and 19,737 children), the bulk of them in 1946. In February 1947, the Immigration Branch inherited the bureau's responsibilities, and by the time the free transportation scheme was over, in March 1948, a grand total of 43,454 women and 20,997 children were brought to Canada.

At the height of the war bride's transport in the summer of 1946, there were offices in four locations: London, The Hague, Paris, and Brussels. Most of the bureau staff were military men with a background in administration and were called upon to do many things that probably were not in the job description when they joined the army. Bureau staff did everything from arranging detailed travel itineraries and passenger sailing lists for women and babies, to booking doctor's appointments and arranging extensions of Dependent's Aid for war brides who were unable to travel; from offering legal advice on custody, to sorting out the marriage problems of wives and husbands: the Canadian personnel of the Wives Bureau had a fascinating and, many times, frustrating job.

The bureau also helped organize war brides' clubs like the Croydon Canucks and Edinburgh War Brides Club. The clubs gave war brides an opportunity to meet each other and to learn about Canada through a lending library, cooking classes, and films. As part of a publicity campaign for the bureau, Mrs. Mona Loosen, wife of Canadian airman Flying Officer Philip Loosen of Bathurst, had her picture taken with a group of other wives looking over a large map of New Brunswick.

The first dedicated sailing under the aegis of the Canadian Wives Bureau took place on February 5, 1946, with the departure of nine hundred dependents from Liverpool on board the *Mauretania*. Called "Operation Daddy" by the Canadian press, the transportation of war brides hit a peak in June and July 1946, when more than six thousand women and children arrived in Canada each month. Every day the Canadian newspapers announced the arrival of another war bride ship, with long lists containing personal details such as the woman's first and

The Wives Bureau organized war bride clubs all over Britain, where women would meet to learn about Canadian life. Here, war brides from the Croydon Canucks War Brides Club gather for a group photo prior to their departure for Canada. Courtesy of Susan Willis

last name, her husband's name and rank, their children's names, and her destination in Canada. In the Saint John *Telegraph-Journal* alone that year, there were an incredible 170 newspaper articles about war brides.

Helping the war brides on their trans-Atlantic journey were members of Volunteer Aid Detachments like the Canadian Red Cross, which supplied Escort Officers (E/Os) to help war brides in the hostels in England and on board ship to Halifax. Among the E/Os were five young women from New Brunswick: Kay (Douglass) Ruddick and Mardy (Holder) Van Der Mude of Moncton, and Marion (Robb) Beattie, Anne (Freestone) Hutchinson, and Elva Ferris from Saint John. They joined more than ninety female volunteers recruited from every province for the sole task of bringing war brides to Canada.

E/Os were officers by rank, but when they worked with the war brides they wore white aprons with the Red Cross emblem emblazoned on the chest. And they did manual labour, feeding hundreds of children and wives, making beds, and tending to the needs of seasick dependents en route to Canada. Twenty-one years old and brimming with excitement at her posting to the Red Cross, Kay Douglass kept a detailed diary of her

A group of war brides, including the late Mona (Ogg) Loosen of Fredericton, gather around a map of New Brunswick at a meeting of the Edinburgh War Brides Club. Courtesy of Iona Loosen

service in 1946. On one of her fifteen Atlantic crossings, Kay was on the *Queen Mary* during a dangerous Atlantic storm:

> Terrific sea: around midnight wave hit the ship and was so huge, splashed in the portholes on top deck and hit the bridge, down the gangway into the Captain's cabin. . . . electrical equipment put out of commission and ship stopped for two hours, bobbing like a cork . . . brides, babies (1,000 brides and 1,000 babies on board) ship's crew all sick all over the place! Men, civilians and other passengers, turned to, to help us look after the babies. By morning the seas had calmed down and the "cleanup" started . . . wet mattresses galore, not to mention gallons of Javex used to clean the cabins and decks.

The Atlantic passage was just the start of a journey that took some war brides to destinations a continent away, but on the whole the process worked seamlessly, and the women and their children were well cared for. The arrangements continued after landing at Pier 21 in Halifax, where the war brides were processed by Immigration officials who stamped their ID cards and sent them along on the next stage of their trip. In a day before four-lane highways, two-car families, and extensive air travel, Canada's vast railway network was used for the onward journey from Halifax. Specially outfitted passenger trains, dubbed "War Bride Specials," departed the siding at Pier 21 for every city, town, and whistlestop across the country.

War brides heading to points in New Brunswick had a short trip, a half-day's travel, and an overnight in Moncton or Saint John, at most, as they waited for connections to rural parts of the province. English war bride Mary (Didlick) Imhoff was eighteen years old and a cook with the ATS when she met Regis Imhoff of Bathurst in 1943. Regis was serving with the North Shore Regiment, and they met at Trafalgar Square in London on a blind date. In early 1945, Regis was wounded, and after he recuperated, was sent back to England, where they were married in

April. When the war ended, Regis was quickly repatriated to Canada. By this time, Mary was pregnant, so she had a long wait before she boarded the *Queen Mary*, more than a year later, on July 19, 1946. Mary recalled her arrival at the train station in Bathurst at one o'clock in the morning, holding their five-month-old daughter, Margaret, whom Regis had never seen. While waiting to get off the train, one of the war brides in the line ahead of Mary was prevented from disembarking because there was no one there to meet her. "I thought, 'Oh, my God, I hope there is somebody there to meet me!' I had the baby in my arms, and I had my luggage, and all of a sudden somebody said, 'Is there anyone there to meet Mrs. Imhoff?' Oh, there was a dozen voices. One grabbed my baby, the other one grabbed my suitcase, and my husband grabbed me."

Further south, at the train station in McAdam, Mrs. Valreia Hunter of the Red Cross Training Meeting Committee waited patiently for the war bride trains and greeted each woman who disembarked at her small town. It was her responsibility to make sure servicemen's dependents were met by the person so named on the passenger lists, and she took her job very seriously. Mrs. Brenda (Rudd) McArthur of Twickenham, Middlesex, came to Canada on the *Mauretania* on February 9, 1946, on the first dedicated sailing of war brides under the auspices of the Canadian Wives Bureau, and there were bound to be some mix-ups. According to the instructions from Red Cross headquarters, Brenda and her three-and-a-half-year-old son, Robert, were supposed to spend the night at the Hunters' house across the street from the station in McAdam. Brenda's husband, Ivan, who had served with the Carleton and York Regiment overseas, was to pick them up the next day. But Ivan showed up unexpectedly to greet his wife, and he booked a room in the Station Hotel. This was contrary to Mrs. Hunter's well-laid plans, and she was reluctant to allow the three of them to spend the night together. But when she asked Robert to identify the man, the small boy said it was his daddy, and that seemed to satisfy Mrs. Hunter.

Mrs. Hunter kept a detailed diary of her train-meeting duties for that year, when the war bride transport was at its peak. In it she recorded the minutest details about the women she met, including Mrs. Jean Paul, an

English war bride who married an Aboriginal soldier from Tobique. Jean (Keegan) Paul was from Coulsdon, Surrey, and was just fifteen years old in 1942 when she met Charles Paul, a status Indian who was overseas with the Carleton and York Regiment. Jean and Charlie fell in love and were married in 1943. If there was ever any racism towards Charlie, none of Jean's family noticed it. In fact, it wasn't until Jean's first child was born in 1944 that the idea of Charlie's being different from other Canadian soldiers even came up in conversation. Jean's older sister, Pat, who still lives in England, commented, "I remember a girl came over to look at Jean's baby, Christine, and said, 'Oh, she's white!' I was amazed. I never even thought of Charlie, or his brother Jim, as not being like us."

In Britain, however, the Red Cross tried to dissuade Jean from marrying a Native Canadian, and so did the padre of Charlie's regiment, but Jean would not hear of it. In New Brunswick, too, people noticed the presence of a young English war bride on the Indian reservation. In the January 1947 minutes of the Perth-Andover Red Cross Society, the Welfare Committee reported that it provided a "layette of 41 pieces ready to go to an English War Bride who married a Maliseet Indian." Jean was the only white woman on the reserve, and conditions were rough. They had no fridge or stove, and the bathroom was an outhouse in the back yard. Rats would scamper across the floor of their shack at night, and the view out the front yard was of the next-door neighbour's pigs. Jean's second-oldest daughter, Cindy, recalls the Indian agent making his annual assessments and dropping off a barrel of flour and leftover army rations for each family. At the Catholic convent school, the nuns gave the children hard tack and cod liver oil to fight off malnutrition and rickets.

Life wasn't easy for Jean and Charlie, but they managed. She never complained to her family back in England, who knew nothing about the challenges she faced in Tobique until many years later, when her mother came to visit. Jean adapted to a dramatically different way of life on the reserve, and she learned how to speak the Malecite language fluently. The family picked blueberries in the summer and potatoes in the fall, fished, and hunted, and Charlie worked as a guide in season. He was good to her, and although the first few years were marked by poverty and struggle, they eventually did very well for themselves. Charlie became involved with the Union of New Brunswick Indians, and they moved to Fredericton in the 1970s, where Jean really came into her own after thirty years on the reserve. They raised six children, all of whom have been successful in their own right. Jean died in 1997, but her memory lives on. In 2004, her grandson, T.J. Burke, became the first Native Member of the New Brunswick Legislature and later Minister of Justice and Corporate Affairs. In December 2005, Burke introduced a motion in the New Brunswick Legislature to officially recognize 2006 as the Year of the War Bride in Canada, sparking a grassroots movement that spread across the country.

Another English war bride who married into a Native family in New Brunswick was Mary (Parr) Palmater of Caterham, Surrey. Mary was eighteen years old when she met Frank Palmater in 1940. Frank was with the Carleton and York Regiment and had joined up in 1939. He was half-Native — his mother was a Mi'kmaq from Eel River Bar, and his father was an American who worked in Dalhousie as a lumber contractor. According to the *Indian Act*, when Frank's mother married a non-Native she lost her status and could no longer live on the reserve, nor could she pass on her status to the children. So when Mary and her four-year-old daughter, Sheila, came to New Brunswick, in May 1946, they came to the town of Dalhousie and the home where Frank had grown up. Frank was working in the woods on a logging drive, so she was met at the train station by her brother-in-law, who stopped and bought some lobster on the way home.

Two days later, Frank arrived, straight from the woods and still in his lumberjack clothes. It was the first time Mary had seen him since he had left for Canada the year before, and he "certainly looked different from the soldier I had last seen," she recalled. That first year they lived at his mother's house and then built their own home in Dalhousie. Mary loved her husband, but she found it hard to get used to the way of life — the outhouse in the yard, the wood stove, and no running water. They used a horse to travel around. "To go get groceries, we would go downtown and tie the horse to a post, and in the winter we used a sleigh. And we would pick up driftwood along the beach for the stove." Mary remembered being so homesick that sometimes she would go down to the shore along the Bay of Chaleur, look out across the water, and wonder if she could find a way to get back home to England. "I would have given anything to go back home," she said, but with no money and a growing family, it was impossible. As the children started to arrive, one after the other, Mary got over her homesickness and settled into her new life in Dalhousie.

Not all war brides married their husbands overseas. Quite a few women, both British and European, came to New Brunswick as fiancées of Canadian servicemen. They had to apply for a visa, each application to be accompanied by a letter from the woman's fiancé confirming that he intended to marry the applicant within a certain amount of time — usually thirty, sixty, or ninety days. Although they could apply to travel on the war bride ships, fiancées were such a low priority for the Wives Bureau that many of them opted for air travel instead. Zoe (Blair) Boone of Aberdeen, Scotland, was so fed up with waiting to be reunited with her fiancé Marshall that, one Tuesday morning in early December 1946, she told her mother she wasn't going to wait any more and was flying to Canada instead. Marshall Boone was from Rowena, a remote farming community near the Tobique Indian Reserve in northwestern New Brunswick. He had gone to England in 1939 with the Carleton and York Regiment and was taken prisoner in Sicily on July 22, 1943. When he was finally liberated from the German POW camp, in May 1945, the military was anxious to send him back to his family in Canada.

Marshall and Zoe had less than four weeks together in May/June 1945, and there simply wasn't enough time to get all the paperwork filled out and arrange for a wedding. Zoe was also still in the WRNS and couldn't just walk away from her duties without a formal discharge. All this took time, and before Zoe knew it, Marshall was gone. Their reunion in Canada would have to wait another eighteen months.

Dot (Upton) Matchett of Leicester, England, did not get married overseas because she and her boyfriend, Blair Matchett, had only been going out for a few months before he was repatriated to Canada. Dot was in the ATS and worked in the kitchen at Aldershot. Blair was with the

Royal Canadian Artillery and was also stationed at Aldershot, waiting to be sent back home to Sillikers, a tiny farming village near Miramichi. They met on a blind date in January 1946, but the idea of getting married wasn't something that they dared talk about before he left in April.

Dot and Blair spent as much time together as they could in those few months, but it wasn't easy — especially after she was promoted to switchboard operator and transferred to the military hospital in Chester, on the border of North Wales and England. Still, they kept in touch by mail and saw each other now and then, but the clock was ticking on Blair's departure to Canada. Dot recalled the day she received word that he was going home: "I got special leave and went down to Aldershot to see him before he left. I remember we were in the canteen at his barracks, both very sad. We talked for a long time and he gave me a small key, told me he loved me, that this was the key to his heart and I would always have it. He gave me his home address in Canada, which was Sillikers, Northumberland County, NB, Canada. Afterwards, I thought, what a funny and small address for such a big country as Canada."

Dot figured that once Blair was back in Canada she would never hear from him again. But when she wrote him a letter, he wrote back, and before too long he asked her to marry him. Dot was still in the army and had to go through a lot of red tape to get her discharge, but she finally did. Next, she had to wait for a space on the war bride ships. Like Zoe, Dot waited and watched while all the married war brides were transported to Canada. By February 1947, both she and Blair had run out of patience, so he told her to "come on the first thing that can bring you over, a boat, plane, or wheelbarrow," and he would pay for it. He sent her the $500 fare, which was a lot of money in those days. On February 22, 1947, she flew to Canada via Prestwick on Trans-Canada Airlines. They were married one week later by Reverend Girdwood at the United Church in Red Bank.

Some fiancées did manage to get onto a liner and come to Canada. Barbara (Miles) Holmes of Newport, Wales, was serving with the ATS Signal Corps in Reigate, Surrey, when she met her husband Norman in 1944. Norman was stationed at Redhill, Surrey, where he worked as a

Spitfire mechanic with an RCAF fighter squadron. They saw each other, off and on, for about a year before he was repatriated to Canada in June 1945. When Norman left, the subject of marriage did come up, but he was worried that Barbara, who had been raised in a Welsh city the size of Saint John, might not like it in rural New Brunswick. He suggested that she come to Canada first to see what it was like. Barbara wasn't going to have anything do to with that. "I wanted to get married," she said. "There was no way I was coming over for a visit!"

So they said their goodbyes in the summer of 1945, and Norman left with a promise to write. He must have had second thoughts on the way back home, because as soon as he arrived in St. Stephen he wrote to her and proposed. "I still have the letter," Barbara smiled. She was an only child, and although her father thought it was wonderful that his daughter would travel halfway around the world to get married, her mother was heartbroken and very bitter. She told Barbara, "If I had known you were going to marry him, I wouldn't have been so nice."

It took nearly two years for Barbara to get her discharge from the army. In April 1947, however, she was on the luxury liner *Queen Elizabeth* en route to Canada. Barbara and Norman were married within a month at "a wee little country church" in Waweig, and she wore a two-piece white French model gown with an ostrich feather on the headpiece. Her fashion taste was a first for the community, and the wedding caused "quite a stir."

During the two years they had been apart, Norman had taken advantage of vocational and technical training benefits offered to veterans by the DVA and had finished mechanics courses in Moncton and Saint John. When Barbara arrived, Norman was doing his apprenticeship at a garage between St. Stephen and St. Andrews. To be close to his work, they settled into a little place in the country with no running water or electricity. It was an isolated spot, and the closest neighbours were the Thomases, who had a farm down the road. Mrs. Thomas took a liking to Barbara and told her that if she ever needed anything to "just stand on the doorstep and 'yoo-hoo' and I'll come." But Barbara said it was quite a distance, so she had to "yoo-hoo pretty hard" to be heard. Her first summer, 1947, was very hot, and Barbara was terrified of the mosquitoes, which were more plentiful and ravenous than those in Britain. "There were hundreds of them, and I'd slam the door and run quick because they'd be around the screen." It took a while for Barbara to settle: after their first child was born, they returned to Wales for fifteen months, but they came back to Canada when Norman was offered a job in St. Stephen. They moved into the village, had another child, and have lived there ever since.

The stereotypical portrait of the war brides is one of happy young women eager to start a new life in Canada, but not every serviceman's wife came to this country with joy in her heart. In New Brunswick alone, we know of at least four widows who made the long trans-Atlantic journey with one goal in mind — to meet her late husband's family and friends. Sylvia (Rusbridge) Dickson of Tide Head was one of two English sisters who came to New Brunswick in May 1945 as widows of Canadian servicemen. Sylvia and her sister, Madeline, were from Worthing in southern England, and they had married two Canadians from the Stormont, Dundas and Glengarry Highlanders, an Ontario infantry unit. Madeline's husband, Charlie Chunn, was from Peterborough, Ontario, and Sylvia's husband, George "Bud" Dickson, was from Tide Head, a tiny community of about four hundred people near Atholville.

The two men became close friends overseas and, tragically, they were killed in the early days of the Normandy invasion. Both men are buried in the Beny-sur-Mer Canadian War Cemetery in France. It was Bud's last wish that, should anything happen to him in France, Sylvia would make the trip to New Brunswick with their children to meet his family. Before he left for D-Day, Bud even made Sylvia's sister Madeline promise to help fulfill that wish, if he should die. Madeline agreed, never believing that both she and her sister would come to Canada as widows — but in May 1945, that's exactly what happened.

The plan was for Sylvia, who had two small boys, and Madeline to meet their husbands' families and to return to England within a year. Little did they know what awaited them in New Brunswick. Before the year was out, both sisters were married — Sylvia to her late husband's

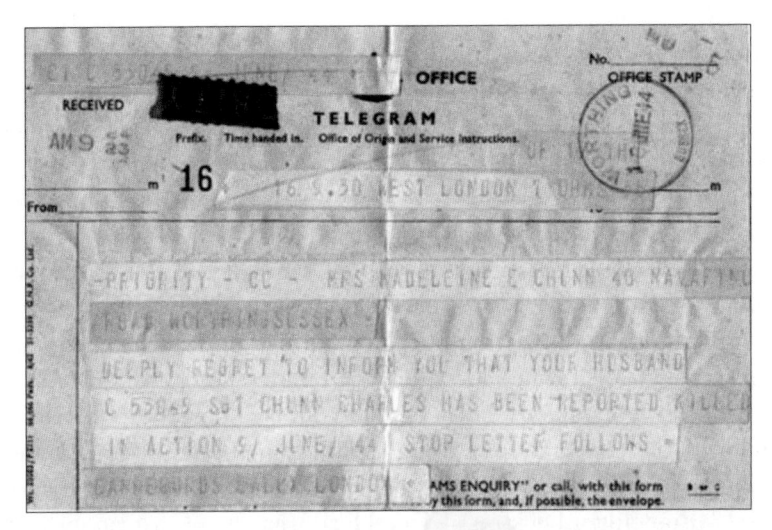

Madeline Fitzgerald's first husband, Charlie Chunn of the Stormont, Dundas and Glengarry Highlanders, was killed in the early days of the Normandy campaign, as was her sister Sylvia's husband, Merle "Bud" Dickson, another Glengarry. The two sisters came to Canada as war widows and found new love in New Brunswick. Courtesy of Madeline Fitzgerald

brother Wallace, and Madeline to a family friend, James "Dewey" Fitzgerald. Both men were overseas veterans and probably never expected to meet, much less to marry, two British war brides in their own hometown. Both sisters raised families and lived in New Brunswick.

The last time English war bride Phyllis (Head) Grover saw her husband Harold was in February 1945, when she waved a tearful goodbye to him on Platform 1 of the railway station in Brighton. Phyllis was from Lewes, East Sussex, and Harold from Fredericton. He had been overseas since August 1940 with the Royal Canadian Artillery and had just been promoted to bombardier, when, as his grandson, Russel Weller, described it, "the good fortune travelling with Harold Grover during the war turned on its heels, packed its bags, and deserted him." Harold's motorcycle was knocked down and he was run over by an armoured personnel carrier in Germany. He died on April 19, 1945 — a mere three weeks before the war ended — and is buried in the Canadian War Cemetery in the village of Holten, the Netherlands.

When Harold died, Phyllis was pregnant with their only child, a daughter she named Haroldene in his memory. In August 1946, when the baby was nine months old, they came to Canada to meet Harold's family in Fredericton. Phyllis and Haroldene spent an entire year in the capital city and it was difficult to leave, but Phyllis knew she had to go back to England. She never remarried, nor came back to Canada again, but her grandson Russel has been to Fredericton many times over the years. Phyllis died in 2005.

Most New Brunswick war brides married soldiers who were stationed in Britain in large numbers, but Scottish war bride Ann (Biles) Johnston's first husband, Ralph Lawrence of Nashwaaksis, was first lieutenant on the Canadian naval destroyer *Athabascan*. They met at the hospital in Mearnskirk, Scotland, where Ann was a nursing sister, and married on April 17, 1944, when Ralph had a forty-eight-hour leave. The best man, Jack Johnston — Ralph's friend from Nashwaaksis — couldn't get leave, so at the last minute he was replaced by Ann's brother. After a twenty-four-hour honeymoon, Ralph had to go back to his ship. Twelve days later, the *Athabascan* was torpedoed by German U-boats and sunk in the English Channel. There were survivors, but Ralph went down with the ship. His body was never found, and he is commemorated on the Halifax Memorial.

Ann was devastated by the sudden and tragic death of her husband. She could not face working at Mearnskirk anymore, so she transferred to another hospital at Barr Hill in southern Scotland. Meanwhile, Ralph's friend, Jack Johnston, starting writing to Ann. Jack was a Canadian Lancaster bomber pilot serving with the RAF and had been awarded the Distinguished Flying Cross. During one of his seven-day leaves, he came up to visit Ann's parents in Glasgow for the week, and on her day off, he went to Barr Hill and spent the afternoon.

In May 1946, Ann was invited to attend the launching of the *Athabascan II* in Halifax. As the widow of a Canadian serviceman, she was entitled to free passage to Canada, so she decided to use the opportunity to meet Ralph's parents in New Brunswick. After the event in Halifax, she took the train to Fredericton and was introduced to Ralph's family and neighbours in Nashwaaksis. Among those who came to meet her was Jack Johnston. Jack was attending the University of New Brunswick, taking a forestry degree on the DVA plan, and Ralph's family played matchmaker, insisting Jack invite Ann to the encaenia. They fell in love, and were married the following year in Fredericton. Both Ann and Jack are gone now: Jack died in 2004, and Ann passed away in 2007.

ଔ

With the fairy-tale weddings and excitement of the ocean journey now behind them, war brides had to face the reality of the lives they had dreamed of in New Brunswick. Some, as indicated here, settled in comfortably and easily; others endured some tough times. British war brides who came to New Brunswick experienced the full range of human emotions, from sadness and joy to resignation and determination. The decisions they made, and how things turned out in the end, were unique to each woman and the challenges she faced. What they all had in common was the willingness to take a chance on a better life in New Brunswick — and if this small sample is any indication, they achieved that goal.

Chapter Three

Settling In

While all war brides would have experienced a period of adjustment — to a new religion, language, or customs — most women coming from urban areas or small villages underwent a major culture shock. After the rosy glow of their reunions wore off, they took a look around and only then realized the full extent of what they had got themselves into in New Brunswick. Winnifred (Green) Keirstead, an English war bride who grew up in London, believed that most soldiers had an idealized, almost romantic vision of the Canada they had left behind in 1939. Whether their descriptions of New Brunswick were misleading by design or they sincerely believed the province was the best place in the world to live, it is impossible to tell.

Certainly, for some soldiers, after six long years away from home, nothing could compare to New Brunswick — at least as they imagined it — and no doubt many painted a rosy portrait of the bucolic splendour of the province. War brides, too, were caught up in some self-deception. They were so much in love and swept up in the mad rush of excitement that they didn't think to ask if everything their husbands said was true. "They told us about Canada," Winnie Keirstead recalled. "What a wonderful country it was, the wide open spaces — but there was a lot they forgot to tell us, and being only eighteen years old it never crossed my mind to ask."

Edith (Dasch) Tompkins (circled) poses with other Red Cross volunteers in a wartime group photo. *Courtesy of Jeannine Rasmussen*

The transition was especially difficult for city girls, used to going to the movies and dances, and hopping on the subway or bus at a moment's notice. In 1946, rural New Brunswick offered primitive transportation, dirt roads, and no electricity or running water in most homes: the building of a province-wide electrical system was a post-war project. Add to that the difficulty of finding work, housing, or child care, and the bitterly cold winter weather, and it's no wonder that some families moved off the farm and into the cities, or out of the province entirely. Some war brides even went back home to Britain and Europe.

Those first few months and years tested the mettle of many relationships. Many war brides moved to towns or cities where their husbands found employment in the natural resources sector, in forestry, fisheries, or mining. Other men couldn't resist the security the military offered, so they gave up struggling on "civvy street," rejoined the army, and ended up in Korea a few short years later.

Every marriage was different: a lot of unions didn't survive the constant upheaval and uncertainty; others thrived upon it. A woman could put up with an awful lot if her husband was good to her and the children. On the other hand, nobody would blame her for walking out when circumstances called for drastic measures. That's what happened to Edith (Dasch) Tompkins, an English war bride who came to Woodstock in 1945. Edith left her husband in 1948. Her daughter, Jeannine, who was two years old at the time, said her mother never spoke about what had happened, other than to say that she couldn't tolerate her husband's drinking, so she just left.

Edith was born in Czechoslovkia and immigrated to England with her parents shortly before the First World War. Her widowed mother was killed in a bombing raid during the Battle of Britain that destroyed their home, so Edith had nobody to return to and nowhere to go when she left her husband. Edith put on a brave face and went looking for work as a live-in housekeeper in the area. She answered a classified advertisement in Anfield, a tiny place near Plaster Rock, and moved there with Jeannine. Edith ended up marrying the man who owned the house, Earlin Tompkins, and they had a child together.

Winnie Keirstead's first husband was from Hardwood Ridge, a small community between Minto and Chipman. He got as far as grade eight before he left school to work in the coal mines at Minto, and when war broke out he joined the army, becoming among the first Canadians to arrive in Britain in December 1939. He served six years in the Carleton and York Regiment and was repatriated to Canada in 1945. Winnie's husband could not make a go of the farm he bought with his DVA re-establishment credits, so after three years he gave up and moved the family to Minto, where he returned to the coal mines. After a stint in Labrador, he rejoined the army, as did many former soldiers who were disillusioned with the reality of civilian life. That brought its own problems for Winnie, who was left behind in Minto with six children to raise on $100 a month.

In the days before social assistance, family allowance, and GST rebates, a woman was financially dependent on her husband; and if he decided $100 was enough for seven people — as did Winnie's husband — then that's what she had to feed, clothe, and house her family for an entire month. Winnie was an extraordinarily resourceful and disciplined person. Diagnosed with tuberculosis and placed in a sanatorium at age five, she was given up by her widowed father and raised in an orphanage from the age of seven. There she learned how to sew clothes like a professional, cook bread and meals from scratch, take care of up to thirty babies at a time in the nursery, and do housekeeping, all skills which came in handy on the farm and later in Minto, when she was all alone with little money and less food.

When others probably would have given up, Winnie persevered; but there was a limit. One particularly disastrous winter, after her husband had rejoined the army, she had completely run out of money, all the children were sick, and Winnie herself was on the verge on pneumonia. Neighbours in Minto came to their rescue, but the respite was only temporary. Winnie's complaint to her husband's commanding officer elicited another $40 per month to support herself and the six children, but it still wasn't enough. She had to take in sewing to make ends meet, and hardship and loneliness were her constant companions.

Winnie and her husband divorced, and in 1961 she moved the children to Fredericton where she started a new life. She re-married, but her second husband, Jerry Waddlow, died suddenly after only five years together. She's been happily married to her third husband for more than forty years and has written a book about her life, *From Grief to Grace*, which describes her childhood in the sanatorium and orphanage, and her arrival in Canada. Underlying her happy disposition is a philosophical outlook based on a strong religious faith that helped her endure those first few years. "Some people get bitter and some people get better," Winnie said of the hardships that came her way. "I chose to be better."

For some war brides, life in rural New Brunswick was a wonderful adventure, and they easily adapted to their new surroundings. After six years of war, these women and their husbands were eager to start anew; and they looked back with fondness, years later, at the simplicity of those early days, the slow pace of life compared to wartime Britain, and how their love for one another and the distractions of a growing family made all the hard times fade away. Annie (Hill) Grant fitted into the mould. She was from Leigh, Lancashire, and served in the ATS as a radar operator with a Heavy Artillery (Anti-Aircraft) Battery. She met Gunner David Grant of the 3rd Anti-Tank Regiment, RCA, when she was on leave visiting her parents in Willingdon, Eastbourne. Annie had grown up in a rural area, so she was right at home at the Grant's family farm in Kilburn, a few miles downriver from Perth-Andover. They had cows, pigs, horses, and chickens, and she wasn't surprised in the least by the lack of such modern amenities as electricity, an indoor toilet, or running water. "I was lucky David had told me about the farm," Annie said. "He said that I would have to pump water, fill all oil lamps, and use a wood stove. In spite of all the differences, ups and downs, all my neighbours and the people I met were so helpful and friendly. I learned how to can vegetables, make a garden, raise a family, and help on the farm."

Other country girls thrived in rural New Brunswick. Isabella (Brand) Anderson came from Glen Tanar, Aberdeenshire, Scotland, to the "gum road" off Bartibogue Bridge, a small settlement near the main road between Newcastle and Bathurst. Her husband Weldon was a woodsman, and when war broke out he joined the Forestry Corps and logged the forests of rural Scotland. Isabella was Protestant, but she converted to Catholicism, and they were married in 1943 when she was just eighteen years old. By the time she arrived in New Brunswick in 1946, she already had three small children, and over the years another twelve would come along, making a total of fifteen children in the large Anderson family. "Luckily, I was a country lass," wrote Isabella of her new life in the backwoods of New Brunswick. "Now my adventures really began."

At first, they lived with Weldon's parents on the family homestead, but then they moved to a house on the "main road" where in addition to the three (and soon to be four) children, Isabella took care of the elderly lady who lived there while Weldon worked in the woods. For Isabella those were happy times, and she can still see him walking to work "with his bucksaw and axe over his shoulder." Later Weldon found work in his trade, building the radar station in St. Margaret's (south of Chatham), so they moved to a house in Redmondville, on the other side of Miramichi, about halfway to Richibucto.

It was simple, country living, and Isabella had no problem making the adjustment, with all the surprises and troubles it could bring. Isabella's nearest neighbours, the Quinns, had a farm and the animals seemed to take a liking to her and the children. "My two little boys used to go every morning to get milk for our family, until one morning Mrs. Quinn's pig got out and chased my boys. It was a big friendly pig, but it surely scared the little lads, and me, too. But I was a real animal lover, so got over the fear for my boys." Another time, the neighbour's horse decided to come for a visit. "Ed Quinn's horse used to always come to my door for a treat. One day I had the front door open and we were eating supper, and we heard the clump, clump coming in the hall looking for a treat. I can hear my husband Weldon saying 'Ella, you and your animals!'" Undaunted, Isabella gave the horse his treat and backed him out of the house like a real pro.

Living in a rural area, in the days before medicare, meant that most of Isabella's babies were delivered at home by itinerant midwives when the country doctor couldn't make it to their house on time. She remembers the night that baby number five was born: "Mrs. Quinn, my good neighbour, never saw a baby being born before, and the baby didn't wait for the doctor to arrive. I can picture Mrs. Quinn yet, by the window, with her prayer beads. Dr. Percy Losier just charged us 'half price' as he was too late. The following year, another little lad arrived. Once again, Mrs. Quinn was with me, and she called the doctor and he came."

Despite the fond memories, Isabella's life wasn't easy. A devastating fire destroyed the old homestead and all their possessions when the youngest child was just two years old. Then Weldon died unexpectedly, leaving her with a large family to take care of on her own. But Isabella's recollections of coming to New Brunswick paint a blissful scene of a self-sufficient, rural life with its seasonal ebbs and flows that has largely disappeared from modern society.

> We always had plenty to eat. Weldon was a great hunter, never shot or trapped more than we needed. He used to poach salmon, then salt them in a big barrel enough to do all winter. It was always "fish on Friday." The moose meat

we used to can. We would build a big fire in the back yard and we would have a big tin bath tub full of water over the fire to put all the canned meat in to cook, usually around 100 cans. We would be up half the night cooking, the children blissfully sleeping. We always had a couple of pigs running around the yard. In winter after they were slaughtered we would hang them in the barn. Lots of hens for eggs and green vegetables in the summer. Plus we picked blueberries, raspberries, strawberries for jams and pies and we were never hungry when the snow whistled around the house.

Isabella Anderson's experiences are typical of many war brides, both British and European, who settled in rural New Brunswick. "I've had many ups and downs," she said, matter-of-factly, "But all in all, I've had a very happy and contented life in Canada."

It was different, however, when a Protestant English war bride ended up in a Catholic, French-speaking community, where religion was an important part of everyday life. One woman who had some adjusting to do was Yvonne (French) Maillet of Ringmer, Sussex. Yvonne was only seventeen years old when she married Flavien Maillet, a French-speaking soldier who was serving with the Carleton and York Regiment. Flavien was from Rogersville, a small village between Moncton and the Miramichi. He was introduced to the family when Yvonne's father, who was the village butcher, met him playing baseball with some soldiers on the Ringmer village green. Yvonne and Flavien became friends and corresponded after he was sent to Italy in 1943. Tragically, Yvonne's father was killed in a bombing raid in 1944 while out on one of his deliveries. When Flavien returned from Italy, he and Yvonne were engaged, and in July 1944 they were married in a Catholic ceremony.

When Yvonne arrived in Rogersville she found out that she was the only war bride in the community and, although Flavien's family could speak a little English, she was surrounded by a sea of French. To complicate matters, his parents were profoundly religious and were quite upset when they found out that Yvonne had not converted to Catholicism. All she had done was promise to raise the children as Catholics, and she had no idea how important that was to her husband's family.

"When I arrived in Rogersville, they made an awful scene that I was not Catholic," said Yvonne. "Every night his parents would say the rosary, and I felt out of place." The priest would visit the house, and they had to hide magazines that he did not approve of. When Yvonne found out she was pregnant with their first child, she decided to take instructions in the Catholic faith, and that seemed to make relations with everyone infinitely better, especially with her mother-in-law. "I think she was very happy that I decided to become a Catholic," said Yvonne, "and I'm sure my husband, too, because he's a devout Catholic as well." Yvonne's husband found work in construction, and they moved to St. Louis-de-Kent and then Fredericton, finally settling in St. Stephen.

Edna (Darby) Blanchette of Shoreham-by-Sea, Sussex, also came to a French-speaking family, this one in Glenlivet, Restigouche County, but for her religion was not the problem. "My first few years were pretty bad," she explained. "Not because of my husband, because of my brother-in-law." Edna's husband Tom had served with the Cameron Highlanders, and when he came back from the war, bringing with him an English war bride and twin boys, his younger brother felt threatened. Soon, Edna found herself in the middle of a power struggle over the family farm.

The situation was complicated because Edna's mother-in-law could not speak English, and since Edna couldn't speak French, she says her brother-in-law "caused a lot of trouble" between the two women. In addition to looking after her own husband and family, Edna had to feed her brother-in-law and wash his clothes. When she asked Tom why she had to take care of his brother, he said "it's between mother and you, and you have to solve it." "He said if I'd learn to stick up to her, answer her back, she'd be fine and friendly," Edna said, "but it was something I had to do myself." After putting up with this for a couple of years, Edna finally had enough and one Sunday morning, "it all blew up! I was feeding the children when my brother-in-law came in and demanded his breakfast.

I asked him to wait while I got the kids settled but he rushed in and told his mother I refused to give him anything to eat. Out she came, heaven only knows what she was saying, I don't, but I got good and mad, told her he was her son and from then on she had him for feeding, washing, and cleaning his room." When Edna took one step towards her mother-in-law, the old lady ran from the room, bolting all the doors behind her. The brother-in-law ran out the other door. "I looked at my husband and he was laughing his head off. That did not make me any happier until he explained: 'From now on you and mother will be the best of friends.' I asked him why she ran so fast," Edna recalled, "and he said he had told her never to make me real mad as I had learned unarmed combat in the army and could throw her over my shoulder."

Two days later, her brother-in-law was out of the house completely and in a place of his own. Edna and her husband stayed and raised ten children on the family farm. When her husband started working as a carpenter, she was left to tend to the farm animals, which at that time was "one cow to milk, one horse to see to, six pigs, and eight hundred chickens." Edna said she "loved every minute of it."

Not every war bride who came to New Brunswick settled here. While some veterans slipped back into positions they had vacated before the war, others could not find steady work in the small communities where they grew up or in the cities where they hoped to live with their new families. An article in the *Telegraph-Journal* in February 1946 summed it all up: "Employment Is Said 'Not Encouraging' for Ex-Servicemen."

Compounding the problem of employment was a serious housing shortage all across Canada, and so it was in New Brunswick after the war. Houses were impossible to rent, and small walk-ups or basement flats were at a premium, no matter where you lived. In Saint John, the *Telegraph-Journal* reported in March 1946, the "Housing Situation for Married Vets Said 'Desperate'." Many war brides ended up living with relatives in cramped houses for longer than they would have liked, and, with an average of five persons per household already, to add a returning soldier, his wife, and a child or two, crowded the existing accommodations — and frayed many nerves.

Some couples took the leap and moved into makeshift houses with no insulation or amenities. One war bride in northwestern New Brunswick lived in a "shack in the middle of a field," where she could see the light shine through the cracks in the walls, and the snow accumulated inside along the window edges and door. "It was all we could get," she remembered, "and we were glad to have it."

Faced with these hardships, many families picked up their belongings and moved to Ontario or out west. But like their modern-day counterparts who have moved away for work, some discovered that the grass was not greener on the other side of the fence; many eventually made their way back home to New Brunswick. English war bride Winifred (Martin) Rutledge came to Doaktown, where her husband Floyd was working in his father's engine repair shop. She liked her husband's family and easily made friends there, but Doaktown was not where she and Floyd were supposed to be. Winifred was a classically trained ballet dancer from Leeds and she was working as a plotter in the Royal Observer Corps when she met Floyd, an engine mechanic in the RCAF. Floyd had gained some notoriety as a nose cone artist during the war: in fact, one of his works, "Fangs of Fire," is in the Canadian War Museum today. When they married, their plan was for Floyd to go to the University of New Brunswick in Fredericton and get a degree in geology, courtesy of the DVA, which offered free university training grants to qualifying veterans. A veteran's village comprised of army H-huts had grown up around Odell Park in Fredericton, and a thriving community took root there. Floyd had actually attended UNB's fall semester in 1945, but when his father became ill, Floyd was needed back in Doaktown to run the shop.

Three years later, his father was well enough to return to work, so Floyd figured he could pick up where he left off and go back to university in Fredericton. But by 1949, Veterans Affairs said he had waited too long to take advantage of the training grants. Floyd appealed to the then Minister of Veterans Affairs, New Brunswick-born Milton F. Gregg, VC, who had recently been president of UNB. Gregg secured permission for Floyd to continue with his studies under the sponsorship of DVA, and he became one of the last veterans to attend university on the free tuition

Winifred and Floyd Rutledge at his graduation from the University of New Brunswick in 1955. Floyd was one of the last veterans to graduate from UNB under the DVA plan. He and his wife credited Milton F. Gregg, VC, a fellow New Brunswicker who was the Minister of Veterans Affairs, for allowing Floyd to continue his studies. Courtesy of Barbara Priestly scheme. Floyd graduated in 1955. "Milton Gregg saved our future," said Winifred. "If it hadn't been for him, Floyd would never have gone back to university, and we probably would have stayed in Doaktown for the rest of our lives."

Floyd and Winifred followed the path of mining exploration, eventually moving to Ontario, where Winifred taught ballet for more than twenty-five years. But, she said, Floyd's "heart and soul was always in the Miramichi," and they returned there often over the years to visit family. Even though Winifred lived in Doaktown only for three years, she made lifelong friends with the war brides there, including Doris (Legate) Amos, who was among the first wives to come to Doaktown in 1944, and twin sisters Mae and Eileen (Goulding) Murray, who married two brothers and settled in the village after the war.

Irish war bride Rose (Connoly) McLenaghan and her husband, Norman, of Baie du Vin, near Miramichi, tried their hand at farming after the war, but the bright lights of St. Catharines, Ontario, beckoned and they left to test their fortunes in the city. Norman had served with the 104th Anti-Tank Battery, RCA, and Rose was a registered nurse who had specialized in psychiatry in England. Rose could easily have found a good job in any hospital, but Norman, like many men of his era, didn't want his wife to work. A daughter, Maureen, came along in 1947, and two years later, they gave up on the idea of farming altogether, sold the house they had bought with Norman's re-establishment credits, and moved to central Canada, eventually making their way to Niagara Falls. But life in Ontario was not all it was made out to be, and soon they returned to Baie de Vin. There they bought a small general store, which they operated for twenty years, and for six years ran the post office in the community.

After selling the store, Rose and Norman moved to Douglastown, now part of Miramichi. They had hoped Norman could retire, but he grew bored of that and found work with the Corps of Commissionaires for another dozen years, while Rose indulged her love of all things Irish by taking part in the annual Miramichi Irish Festival. When Rose passed away, in 1991, the priest said at her funeral: "She was known by all, from the head of the tide to the farewell buoy."

Other couples tried their luck in the United States. English war bride Eileen (Meaden) Mesheau arrived in Salisbury, outside of Moncton, on March 6, 1946, six months pregnant and "the worse for wear" after ten days on board the *Letitia*. When told where she was headed, one of the ship's crew exclaimed, "You poor bugger, that's not even in Canada!" Husband Bill Mesheau found employment in Moncton with the passenger bus company SMT Eastern as a driver. Housing was difficult to get in Moncton, so they rented a small house in Salisbury, where, much to Eileen's displeasure, they only had an outhouse. "It almost turned me off of New Brunswick," Eileen said. "If you had a child or were pregnant, forget it, nobody would rent you a place, and you couldn't get a wartime house unless you had two children."

After the birth of their second child, they moved to Moncton, where they qualified for veteran's housing at a cost of $32 a month. During this time Bill was hired by John Deere Tractors as a manager of the Moncton Branch. In 1959 John Deere laid off all its managers, and Bill and Eileen decided to try their luck in Massachusetts, where Bill had relatives. He ended up owning and running a successful business in Ludlow, near Boston, and except for a nine-year stint in Ottawa, they have lived there ever since.

English war bride Betty (Lowthian) Hillman was from Newport, Isle of Wight, off the southern coast of England. She was sixteen years old and working as an Academy Girl dancer in an entertainment troupe called Concert Party when she met her husband, Doug Hillman, who was serving in the Provost Corps. After the war, she came to an isolated farm in Hawkins Corner near Millville, which her husband shared with his brother and elderly uncle. Betty had to overcome her fear of cows, crows, and bears, and learn how to draw water from a nearby stream. But she never got used to the little minnows that she could see swimming around in the bucket of drinking water.

After Betty became pregnant with their first child, Doug sold eight

Betty (Lowthian) Hillman was a member of the Academy Girl dance troupe on the Isle of Wight. She met her husband Doug when she was sixteen years old, and they married when she was eighteen. Courtesy of Betty Hillman

pigs to buy her a ticket back home to the Isle of Wight. He joined her some months later, and they lived in England for twelve years before coming back to New Brunswick. Betty's husband passed away in 1987, and she went to live with her daughter in Upper Kintore, near Perth-Andover.

Most war brides will admit to a few episodes of homesickness, but for some it was unbearable, especially if the woman was too proud to admit that her fairy-tale romance had not turned out as planned in Canada. Social expectations of married women in the post-war years made divorce unthinkable, and a common expression was "You made your bed, now you have to lie in it." English war bride Doris (Farrow) Marks fell into that category. She came from Roffey, Horsham, Sussex, to Miscou Island, a remote fishing community off the northeastern corner of the province, at the entrance to Chaleur Bay. Doris's husband had served with the North Shore Regiment overseas, and was from an English family in the mainly French-speaking community.

Doris didn't know very much about Miscou except what her husband had told her. "He said it's a beautiful place at night with the stars and the moon reflected in the water, but he didn't tell me about the lack of running water, the outhouse, or no electricity," Doris recalled. "I came to a very poor house," Doris said, but she quickly pointed out that it was like that for everyone in Miscou after the Depression and the war. The only way on and off the island was by ferry in season, and by ice highway in winter. There was a Red Cross nursing station where you could get minor injuries tended, and sometimes a nurse could deliver a baby. But if you needed a doctor, you had to go to the mainland.

One time, Doris went with the nurse to assist a pregnant English war bride on a neighbouring island who was about to deliver a baby. "She wanted me to be there. I suppose she felt better having an English person there while she had her baby." But when Doris arrived at the war bride's house, she was shocked by the condition the woman and her children were in. "It was absolute poverty," Doris recalled. Doris's husband had work as an assistant lighthouse keeper and did some fishing like most

Settling In | 77

other men on the island. They may not have been rich but "we always had plenty to eat," she remembered.

Still, Doris just couldn't adjust to life on Miscou Island. "I was so homesick," she recalled of those first few years. "You couldn't say there was anything the same as home, because there wasn't." Doris would take the two dogs down to the shore, sit on a rock, and cry. "I cried buckets when I came here, and when the tide came in, I used to say it was five feet higher because of my tears."

Doris's unhappy state did not go unnoticed by her husband. In 1949, he bought her a ticket to England. Doris never told her mother what was happening in Canada, because "she had enough worries of her own." Besides, Doris's mother had disapproved of the marriage from the beginning, and Doris didn't want her to say "I told you so." Doris spent six glorious months in England, going to the movies and theatre, soaking up all the things she couldn't do on Miscou. She even found a job, but towards the end of the six months, her mother finally asked, "Don't you think you should be going home to your husband? That's your place," her mother said. "You have to go back."

Doris wanted desperately to stay in England. She had no children and could easily have made a life for herself there, but to do so would be to admit defeat. So she returned to Miscou. She and her husband had two boys, but the marriage didn't last. They divorced, and she remarried another man from the island, with whom she had a daughter. Except for a period when she left her first husband, she continued to live in Miscou. Despite everything, Doris figured she had it better than some of the other English war brides who came to the area. And even though she did not like Miscou Island at first, she grew to "love it."

Some war brides never really overcame their homesickness. Hilda (Jones) Jenkins Jarvis and her four-week-old daughter, Elaine, arrived at her father-in-law's house in Burnt Land Brook, nine miles from Plaster Rock, at 2:00 o'clock in the morning on December 19, 1946. When she woke up, the view out the window was of a solitary pine tree in the middle of a field of snow. She told her husband she "didn't like it," and his response was, "once you get to know the people, you'll feel differ-

Hilda (Jones) Jenkins Jarvis with her daughter, Elaine, at the rooming house in Sussex where she lived while her husband was in the sanatorium with tuberculosis. Hilda spent much of her first two years in Canada alone, because of her husband's illness. Courtesy of Hilda Jenkins Jarvis

ent." But it wasn't so simple. Hal Jenkins had been with the Argyll and Sutherland Highlanders of the 5th Canadian Division, and was seriously injured in Bergen op Zoom, Holland. He then developed tuberculosis, so when Hilda arrived in New Brunswick from Slough, England, he was in a sanitorium in Sussex. They had two weeks together in Burnt Land Brook that Christmas, but then Hal had to go back to the sanatorium. Hilda was left behind amidst the snow and isolation of rural New Brunswick, and by February she'd had enough. She moved to Sussex with Elaine so they could be closer to Hal, and when he was transferred to the hospital in Saint John, they moved there, too. Hilda spent much of her first two years in Canada alone with her daughter, and she recalled being so homesick that she was almost "ashamed" of herself.

Settling In | 79

Dot (Upton) Matchett came to Canada as a fiancée and married her husband, Blair Matchett, within a week of arriving in New Brunswick. Courtesy of Dot Matchett

If laughter is the best medicine, then that was the tonic on which all the war brides relied to make it through the tough times. They could entertain any listener with hilarious incidents that occurred as a result of their complete ignorance of country life, or when they used an expression that had an entirely different meaning in New Brunswick. Dot (Upton) Matchett arrived in Newcastle on a cold February day, and in the long taxi drive home to Sillikers her husband put the window down to let in some fresh air. Dot asked him if he could please roll up the window, because the wind was ruining her "quiff" or hairdo. She could tell by the stunned look on her husband's face and the snickers from the driver that she said something wrong, but she didn't know what it was. Later she found out that "quiff" was local slang for a woman's private parts, and she never used the word again.

More than one British war bride made the mistake of calling her mother-in-law "homely" — a term of endearment in Britain that meant she was loving and kind. In Canada, of course, it was an insult that meant a woman was plain and unattractive. Another common expression that left a few war brides blushing was "Knock me up in the morning." To the British, it meant to be woken up, but to New Brunswickers, being "knocked-up" meant to get pregnant. Imagine a woman announcing to a room full of guests, as she headed to bed for the night, that she'd like to be "knocked up in the morning" — and the whole room breaking out in fits of laughter.

Wedding and baby showers were unheard of in Britain, and many war brides were left scratching their heads when told by well-meaning relatives that they were organizing a "shower" to celebrate her marriage or the birth of a child. One woman thought it was some kind of Canadian initiation rite to get doused with water, so she came to her shower prepared with a spare set of clothes.

Other simple *faux pas* derived from unfamiliarity with routine chores. Edna Blanchette remembered one day when her husband told her to burn the softwood first. She went out, felt the wood, and when she came back in, she announced that it all felt hard to her. "Did he ever laugh at me over that!" The challenges of cooking on a wood stove, combined with unfamiliar ingredients and recipes in the hands of city girls who had little experience in the kitchen, resulted in more than one culinary disaster, from bread so hard you could use it for hockey pucks — another expression that required explanation — to chickens that did not cook because the fire was never set. Then there was the woman who went out to get rhubarb and ended up with a burdock pie. She never lived that one down.

☙

Although it took some British war brides a while to adjust to their new lives in New Brunswick, most women eventually did settle in and grow to love it here. Having survived the Depression and the Second World War, there was little that could faze them now. The cultural values they brought to Canada — the stereotypical stiff upper lip and British resolve never to give up — eased their transition into New Brunswick society, and these values never left them entirely. Anyone who has seen the Fredericton Singing War Brides knows, when they sing "You'll Get Used To It," that British stoicism remains a strong part of their character.

But no matter who they were or where they went, once war brides arrived in New Brunswick they all had to decide whether this was the place they wanted to spend the rest of their lives. For some, the decision was out of their hands: traditional attitudes towards marriage and family and personal circumstances made it impossible to change the cards life had dealt them. For others, New Brunswick was one big happy adventure, and they never looked back on the life they left behind in Britain.

Fewer war brides came to New Brunswick from continental Europe, and they form a much less homogenous group. Moreover, their wartime experiences were fundamentally different from those of their British counterparts. Their contributions to the war brides story are among the most compelling.

Chapter Four

Continental War Brides

Canadian servicemen married nearly three thousand war brides from continental Europe and, although we do not know the exact number of these women who made their way to New Brunswick, it is likely no more than one hundred did so. The wartime experience of continental wives was entirely different from that of their British counterparts. The long years of German occupation, the excitement of the Liberation that followed, and the comparatively brief length of time that the Canadians were stationed in Europe are unique to their story. Moreover, while European wives had to make the same adjustments as British women to life in New Brunswick, they had little in common culturally with their husband's relatives, friends, and neighbours. Most were not fluent in English or French, so the need to master a new language was understood from the start. Additionally, a continental war bride was often the sole European-born female in the entire community, so she had to accept the fact that the only person who really understood what she had been through during the war was her husband. Depending on what kind of a man he was, and whether the family and community were supportive or not, her adaptation to New Brunswick could go either way.

Although Canadians served in Italy from July 1943 until March 1945, the vast majority of European war brides came from Northwest Europe, primarily Holland and Belgium. The comparative dearth of Italian war brides was explained by several factors. During the early months of the campaign, Italy was still an enemy state and fraternizing was frowned upon. There were also a vast cultural difference between Canadian soldiers and the deeply impoverished rural peasants of southern Italy as well as a major language barrier that militated against easy liaisons. In the end, only twenty-six Italian women came to Canada as war brides, only one of them to New Brunswick. Language often presented a problem in Northwest Europe as well, but the cultural differences were less and the opportunities better for developing friendly relations with the locals. By 1944, with the end of the war in sight, it was only natural that romance would blossom between the liberators and the liberated.

This was especially true in Holland, which was largely liberated by the Canadian army, and where the army was garrisoned in 1945-46 as it awaited repatriation. The summer of 1945 was notable for both the amount of Canadian servicemen still in the country and the number of women they married. In December 1946, Canada's Immigration Branch reported that wedding bells had rung for 2,667 continental war brides: 649 Belgian, 100 French, 6 German, and 26 Italian. All the rest, 1,886, were Dutch, and Selma (Kater) Smith was one of them.

Selma was twenty years old when the Nazis invaded Holland. Her parents had divorced in 1930, and when her mother died, in 1939, she and her older brother, Albert, and younger sister, Hetty, went to live with their father and his second wife in Amsterdam. The three Kater children, now young adults, had been raised as Christians by their mother, but their father was Jewish. That spring, the air was thick with rumours of invasion, and everyone knew that the cities and seaports would be targets. So Selma, Albert, and Hetty went against their father's wishes and moved to Doorn, a small village located between Utrecht and Amersfoort. Whether he hoped their presence would protect him from the Nazis or he just wanted his children nearby is unclear. Mr. Kater was very angry with them for leaving, calling them "rats fleeing a sinking ship."

Selma, Albert, and Hetty kept a low profile in Doorn. Albert served in the Dutch military until it was disbanded after the invasion and, like many young men, he went into hiding to avoid being conscripted into forced labour camps. Meanwhile, Selma continued working in an office in Amsterdam, travelling daily, until the trains were no longer running. As in all of Holland, their situation was desperate during the "hunger winter" of 1944-45. People starved to death, and Selma was grateful for her share of the hard tack and lard distributed to the population by British soldiers. Fortunately, the Katers survived the war untouched, and the family eventually reconciled.

After Liberation in May 1945, the British in the Doorn area were replaced by Canadians, who set up headquarters in Amersfoort about twenty kilometres away. One day, Selma was walking down the street when she saw a Canadian soldier with a newspaper under his arm. Selma could read a bit of English, so she asked to borrow his paper. Thirty-year-old Sidney Smith was from Upper Mills, near St. Stephen, and was serving with the 36th Battery, 23rd Field Regiment, RCA. He gave Selma the paper and walked her home, so he could bring her "more newspapers tomorrow." They were married in Doorn on a rainy Friday, December 13, 1945: "For superstitious people double trouble," Selma later wrote in her diary, but "it all turned out very well."

Sidney was repatriated in early 1946, and arrived in New Brunswick ahead of Selma. From the time he landed home, he sent letter after letter to her; she kept them in a little box that her daughter, Rose Burke, inherited when she died. Written on Canadian army letterhead, Sidney's writings are filled with undying protestations of love. In one, dated February 26, 1946, he responds to her concerns that some Canadian soldiers were asking their Dutch wives for a divorce. Sidney assures Selma that he would never ask for a divorce and calls her "Dear" seventeen times and "Darling" twelve times, and tells her twice that he loves her so much he "could faint." "I love you so much dear when I think that you may change your mind about coming to Canada it makes me nearly sick enough to faint, that is how much I love you dear. I shall never get along without you."

Selma was five months pregnant when she finally arrived in Halifax on May 23, 1946. She took the train to Saint John, then a bus to St. Stephen, where she was met by Sidney and his parents, and a taxi the

CANADIAN LEGION WAR SERVICES

poststempel 3/3/'46 Fredericton

Upper Mills
Feb 24/46 Char Co.
New Brunswick

Dear Sweetheart just a few lines to let you know I am still living and as well as ever dear I got two of your very welcome letters today one was dated Feb 13 and one the 15th and I was very glad to get them dear and you tell Betty not to be angry and when we are together and get settled we will make it up to her for all she has done for us. and we can get many things here that is impossible to get over there. well darling you say many of the boys are asking for a divorce and many of the girls do not wish to come to Canada. I hope you do not change your mind dear about coming and never fear of me asking for a divorce for I would rather die then to have anything happen between us I love you so much dear when ever I think that you may change your mind about coming to accept, it makes me nearly sick enough to faint that is

PLEASE USE BOTH SIDES

Sidney Smith was repatriated to Canada four months ahead of his wife, Selma (Kater), a Dutch war bride who eagerly awaited transport to Canada. This letter was one of many he wrote to Selma during their separation. *Courtesy of Rose Burke* eight kilometres to Upper Mills. By then Selma was so tired she had trouble following the conversation, peppered as it was with colloquialisms like "upriver" and "downtown." When they finally arrived at the family home, the house was a mess — Sidney had forgotten to let the tomcat out before they left, and it had wreaked havoc with the welcome cake and curtains. Selma did not care; she just wanted to go to bed. But Sidney's mother had one more thing to do before the night was over — introduce Selma to the "two-holer" in the backyard.

That spring and summer, Selma and Sidney lived with his parents in St. Stephen, and when fall came they moved into a rambling old house in Upper Mills. It was uninsulated, and there was no indoor plumbing, but they were happy to be together on the farm where there was peace and quiet after so many years of war. Their first child, a son, was born in August 1946. A daughter arrived the following July, and in September 1947, Selma's sister Hetty immigrated to Canada with her husband, settling in St. Stephen. Later, Albert and his family also came to Canada. Having relatives close by made adapting to rural New Brunswick easier for Selma, who was a city girl unused to the farming life. Selma and Sidney lived the rest of their lives in Upper Mills.

Dutch war bride Elizabeth (van Gervan) LeBlanc came to Chartersville, a small community that is now part of Dieppe, near Moncton. Elizabeth met her husband in Eindhoven after Liberation, and since he was stationed in the area they were never apart for long. Her parents were "very upset" when they found out she was getting married, but she considered herself "rather liberated" and on May 3, 1946, married Trooper Ernest LeBlanc of the 8th Princess Louise's (New Brunswick) Hussars. Elizabeth never considered her marriage to the handsome young Canadian a serious risk: she always knew that, if she didn't like it in New Brunswick, she would be welcome back home with her parents in Eindhoven.

Elizabeth arrived in Chartersville in October 1946, and to her surprise, on one side of the road everyone was French, and on the other side they were English. She could speak four languages, English, French, German, and Dutch, so language was never a problem. Elizabeth was lucky in other ways, too. She and her husband had no problems getting housing, he found steady work at the CNR, and he was good to her; so she stayed in Chartersville her entire life.

Although Elizabeth LeBlanc had an easy transition to New Brunswick, she had a Dutch friend, Janneke (a pseudonym), whose tragic story appears to be right out of a movie script. Before the war, Janneke married a German doctor and they lived in Hamburg with their little girl. When war broke out, Janneke's husband was sent to Poland, and she never heard from him again. Not knowing whether he was dead or alive, she stayed in Hamburg with his mother. Janneke's husband had a friend who was in the Gestapo (the Nazi secret police), but as it turned out, he was a double agent working for the Russians. In a decision she would regret for the rest of her life, Janneke agreed to take a train to Leipzig and deliver some papers, travelling with strict instructions to destroy everything if the Germans stopped the train. As fate would have it, she was caught and sent to a concentration camp. At the end of the war, Janneke was liberated and tried to get back to Germany to find her daughter, but the neighbourhood where the grandmother lived had been bombed and the family was nowhere to be found. When she checked with the Red Cross, they told Janneke the child had gone missing in an Allied bombardment.

With nobody left to remind her of the past and nothing to lose, Janneke married a Canadian soldier. She came to New Brunswick as a war bride and they adopted a baby boy. When the child was five years old, the Red Cross contacted Janneke to say they had found her German husband, their daughter, and his mother. He had been captured by the Russians and forced to train Russian doctors. Janneke's first husband wanted her to come back to Germany, but by this time she was very attached to her new family, especially her little boy. "I do not need to tell you the trauma this caused," Elizabeth wrote, adding that Janneke was never happy again. She died in the early 1980s. "This is just one story but there are many," Elizabeth said.

Dutch war bride Maria (Egbars) Ouellette met her husband Jean-Marie ("John") in December 1944, after Canadian troops took over from the Americans where she lived in Ravenstein, Holland. Maria came from an upper-middle-class family: her father was a successful entrepreneur, and his family owned five hotels. Maria grew up in Utrecht and Eindhoven, and when her parents separated in 1932, the children moved with their mother back to her parents' home in Ravenstein. When the Nazis invaded Holland in May 1940, Maria was only sixteen years old. The first thing that happened was that the schools closed and Maria could no longer attend classes. She was sent out to work in a forced labour gang with other girls and women, peeling potatoes for the German army.

The German occupation was not a happy time for Maria's family. Her brothers had to go into hiding, and food was scarce. Then, in September 1944, American paratroopers landed in Ravenstein and later that fall were replaced by Canadians. Among them was Sergeant Major John Ouellette of the North Shore Regiment. John was a French-speaking soldier from Bathurst, and like many Acadians from northern New Brunswick, he spoke English as well. Her brother met John first and brought him home to meet the family. Maria couldn't speak English or French, and John could not speak Dutch, but they managed to communicate with a sort of sign language.

The war was far from over in the fall of 1944, and the men had to continue fighting, but John kept in touch with Maria. After the war, he stayed on with the army of occupation. It took several months of letter writing to get all the paperwork in order, but when John's permission finally came in, they were married just two days later, on April 3, 1946. John was repatriated in May, and Maria was supposed to come over in July, but she forgot to put "New Brunswick' on her application form to the Wives Bureau in the Hague and all the paperwork came back. On November 4, Maria was among a group of Dutch war brides who sailed from the Hook of Holland to Liverpool. She spent a few nights at the war brides' hostel in London and then boarded the *Lady Rodney* — a small pre war liner used for the Canada-Caribbean route — where she joined a group of thirty-two women from Northwest Europe, three of whom were headed to New Brunswick.

Canadian combat troops spent comparatively less time in Belgium, liberating the western and northern portions of the country, including Antwerp, in late 1944, before passing through to spend the winter in Holland. Nevertheless, the army's logistical tail passed through Belgium, and Antwerp remained a popular leave destination. Alice (Rondeau) Tranquilla of Couillet, Belgium, met her husband, Jim, on Christmas Eve, 1944, when her mother insisted that she invite a Canadian serviceman to their home for Christmas supper. Alice was a university-educated teacher who taught French in a private school during the war years. She had planned to get a teaching degree at Mons University and then continue on to law school at Liège. However, after the Germans invaded on May 10, 1940, the university was closed; there would be no law school in Alice's future.

In 1987, Alice wrote her life story. In this excerpt, she describes the circumstances of that fateful meeting on Christmas Eve, 1944. It was a sombre Christmas. The Germans had broken the Allied lines in the Ardennes forest of southeastern Belgium, in the famous Battle of the Bulge, and an air of apprehension gripped the season.

> The Canadians are with us and for the people of Maman and Mémère's generation, they bring back the memories of yesteryear. They have retreated from the Ardennes, taking with them only their rifle and the uniform on their back. The town opens its heart, families open their homes for Christmas. I myself have to fill the application and Mémère urges me to put in our name but only on the afternoon of the 24th do I unwillingly make my way to the school and place our invitation. At this late date, almost every man who wished it, is booked and the guard tells me he'll inquire at roll-call. When I go back, I am given a bit of paper 'Tranquilla G60853.'

A rare photograph taken from the deck of the *Lady Rodney* by Alice (Rondeau) Tranquilla, as she embarked from Antwerp for Southampton, en route to Canada, September 1946. Dockside farewells were forbidden in Britain, so families had to say their goodbyes at home or in the train station where war brides gathered before going to the hostels. This photo shows Alice's mother, Adolphine Latteur, and Alice's best friend, Camille, as they wait for the ship to depart. Courtesy of Alice Tranquilla

Jim was from Millville, a tiny farming community about sixty kilometres from Fredericton. His family were of Italian descent, and his father worked as an engineer on the railway. Jim originally went overseas with the Forestry Corps, but as reinforcements were needed in 1944, he was moved to France and attached to an American unit in the Battle of the Ardennes. On Christmas Eve, he met Alice in Couillet. They planned to marry the following December 1945, but he came down with diphtheria and didn't show up for the wedding. A month later, Jim had fully recuperated and they staged the wedding again — minus the food and drink that had been used up by the guests the first time around.

Alice's journey to Canada began in Antwerp, where she sailed on the *Lady Rodney* to Southampton. At Southampton she boarded the *Aquitania*, and finally, on September 4, 1946, she arrived in Millville. Alice's transition to life in New Brunswick was not easy. The language, weather, completely different customs, and isolation made her terribly homesick, and she had second thoughts about her decision to leave Belgium. But her love for Jim kept her in Millville. They had five children, and in the 1960s, Alice went back to work teaching French, a rewarding career that brought her back to Europe many times as an escort on student trips. She and Jim continued living in Millville, in the old farmhouse they bought in 1947.

In the passenger lists of the Canadian Wives Bureau, there is a record of one French war bride, Mrs. Suzanne LeBlanc, wife of Sapper J.A. LeBlanc of Lewisville, NB, who came to New Brunswick in September 1946. At first glance, it seems surprising that so few French war brides married New Brunswickers, given that the North Shore Regiment was among the first to land in France on D-Day, and many of those men spoke French. The fact is, however, the fighting in Normandy was intense and virtually continuous for Canadians. French civilians were either evacuated or sheltered in their cellars: there was little opportunity and it was too dangerous to fraternize. Once the Normandy stalemate broke, the Canadian army raced through northern France in a matter of weeks, pausing only to liberate port cities, before settling down again to another long fight in northern Belgium and the Netherlands.

It seems that Canadian soldiers were just too busy to make time with French women in 1944. The same is true of Italy, where there were plenty of New Brunswickers, including the Carleton and York Regiment, the 8th Hussars, the 8th Battery from Moncton, and the 90th Battery from Fredericton, plus all the New Brunswickers in other units. Yet only one New Brunswick serviceman married an Italian war bride, and he was an Irish-Acadian soldier who had originally signed up with the North Shore Regiment.

Twenty-three-year-old Anna Perugine met Sergeant Aurele Lavigne of Bathurst when he went looking for translators to help at Canadian Headquarters in Avellino. Anna came from a prominent family. Her father was a respected surgeon who corresponded with well-known anti-Fascist intellectuals, and they lived in a beautiful home with servants. Her brother was a doctor, and it was expected that all her siblings would attend university. In fact, Anna was taking English at the University of Naples when the war broke out, but after her father died unexpectedly in January 1940, she returned to Avellino to be with her widowed mother. The family suffered greatly during the war: their apartment was bombed out, their belongings were stolen by the Germans, and they had to flee

Anna (Perugine) Lavigne of Bathurst was one of only twenty-six Italians to marry Canadian servicemen during the Second World War. In this photo, taken by a street photographer, the couple walk down a street in Naples, just after the wedding ceremony. Aurele's belongings, including his uniform, had been stolen, so he wore his brother-in-law's dress suit, with the legs a couple of inches too short. Courtesy of Anna and Aurele Lavigne to the mountains for safety. When the Americans landed, in October 1943, things started to return to normal. Then came the Canadians and Sergeant Aurele Lavigne.

Aurele spoke no Italian and Anna could not speak English very well, but she was determined to learn, and she carried a little dictionary everywhere she went. When Aurele was moved out of Avellino, they communicated by letters which Anna's priest helped her to read and write. Aurele had to go through layers of bureaucracy to obtain his commanding officer's permission to marry, but they were married, finally, in Naples in June 1946.

Anna came to Canada on the *Lady Rodney* that November, on the same passage as Maria Ouellette. At first she and Aurele settled in Shippegan. Its wooden sidewalks and dirt roads must have been a complete culture shock to this well-bred young Italian woman, but Anna adjusted well. They ran a general store in the 1950s, until Aurele found steady work in insurance and they moved to Bathurst, where they raised six children.

One of the most extraordinary stories to come out of the European continent involves a young Jewish woman from Vienna. Dorrit (Hacker) Nash's hair-raising escape from the Nazis after the Austrian *Anschluss*, and her marriage to a Black soldier from Lakeville Corner, give her a special place in the history of Canada's war brides.

The Hackers had lived a comfortable, middle-class life in Vienna until German troops entered Austria on March 12, 1938. On that day, life changed forever for fourteen-year-old Dorrit. "That year is best to be forgotten," She wrote in a diary she kept of her wartime experiences. One of the first things the Nazis did was pass anti-Jewish legislation forbidding Jews from attending school or even sitting on park benches. Dorrit had hoped to follow in her father's footsteps and become an accountant, but it was not to be. "Suddenly, I was not allowed to return to school because I happened to be Jewish." In November 1938, came *Kristallnacht* — the infamous "Night of Broken Glass" — when virtually every synagogue in Vienna was burned to the ground. Eventually all Jewish businesses were destroyed, and Jews were rounded up and deported to concentra-

Dorrit (Hacker) Nash was a fifteen-year-old Austrian-Jewish schoolgirl when she was rescued from the Nazis by the *Kindertransport*. She spent the war years in Britain and became a "Rosie the Riveter." When she was nineteen years old, she met Hedley Nash, a Canadian serviceman who was a descendent of Black Loyalists and Malecite Indians. Dorrit and Hedley lived on Fredericton's north side and were the "first" in many respects. Courtesy of Deby Nash

Continental War Brides | 95

tion camps and ghettos in the east. Between 1938 and 1940, an estimated 117,000 of Austria's 192,000 Jews fled for safer shores. Desperate to find any way out of the country, many of them emigrated to Palestine, Britain, and North America.

Jews were not always welcome in foreign countries, and it was extremely difficult to obtain an entry visa. Many families were torn apart when precious visas sent mothers, fathers, and children off in different directions. And so it was with the Hackers. Dorrit's mother, Irma, secured a visa to work as a domestic in England — a major step down in social standing, but given the circumstances, she had no choice. Irma left her husband and daughter behind in Vienna, fully intending to be reunited with them in England at a later date.

As talk of war began to escalate and the more punitive effects of Nazi anti-Jewish legislation started taking effect, Dorrit's father obtained a visa for Palestine and left on board a refugee ship. Dorrit went to live with her paternal grandmother in Baden, outside of Vienna, until she could be smuggled out. In England, Irma made contact with the Jewish Aid Committee organizing the *Kindertransport* — the transportation of ten thousand Jewish children to Britain from German-controlled Europe. Plans were carefully put into place, and after many months of anxious waiting, Dorrit was brought to England as a child refugee, in early September 1939, just as war broke out. She joined her mother in domestic service. "That type of work was totally unfamiliar to me," Dorrit wrote of her first job in England, but at least they were safe — or as safe as one could be in London, given the daily bombing raids during the Battle of Britain.

War work was compulsory, and although Dorrit wanted to join the ATS, she was refused because of her age. Instead, she was referred to a training centre where she learned how to do metal work and gas welding. Dorrit eventually found employment welding tailpipes on fighter airplanes. "The work was very hard," Dorrit wrote in her diary. "Night shifts were especially rough, having to lay on my back with a burning hot blow torch, tacking together large pieces of metal. Outside the air-raid sirens were howling, and bombs were being dropped all around me."

But the worst was yet to come. In October 1941, the Nazis began to systematically round up all the Jews in Vienna, and Dorrit received news that both grandmothers and an uncle had been deported. Another uncle hanged himself rather than die at the hands of the Nazis.

Despite the bombing raids, hard work, and terrible news coming from Europe, Dorrit was still a teenager. What little free time she had was spent at the movies and dance halls. Dorrit seemed to drift towards Black soldiers, perhaps because they, too, were outsiders in Britain. They didn't seem to care about her German accent, or the slight facial paralysis from childhood encephalitis that made her self-conscious every time she smiled. London's Trocadero nightclub was frequented by Black soldiers, and Dorrit often went there with a girlfriend. Her observations of the Black soldier community in London make fascinating reading. She clearly felt accepted by these men and had many platonic friendships. But it was Hedley Nash of Lakeville Corner who captured her heart.

Hedley was a descendent of Black Loyalists — African slaves who fought on the side of the British during the American Revolutionary War. His ancestors had come to New Brunswick in the 1780s and settled in Lakeville Corner, near Grand Lake. His mother, Amy, was a Malecite Indian; so he was half-Black and half-Native. When the shy refugee from Vienna told him she was Jewish, "he couldn't have cared less."

Hedley's family was poor and lived in a falling-down shack with no heat, plumbing, or electricity, but that wasn't the story Hedley painted for his Austrian bride. He told her he owned a successful garage business — in reality, it was a small operation run by two of his nine brothers. Hedley also told Dorrit they were the same age — a lie which came to the surface on their wedding day, in June 1945. It was only as he entered his birth date on the official certificate that Dorrit learned he was twelve years older than he had said. Dorrit's mother Irma, who was witness at the ceremony, never forgave Hedley for that lie. Not an auspicious start to a marriage that, even in the best of circumstances, would have plenty of obstacles to overcome.

Hedley was repatriated to Canada in September 1946. Dorrit and five-month-old baby Diane followed him on the *Empire Brent* in

October. For the first few months, they lived with his parents in Lakeville Corner. Then they moved to Fredericton, where Hedley found work at the Chestnut Canoe Factory. After their third daughter, Deby, was born in 1952, Dorrit's mother Irma moved to Canada to be near her only child and three granddaughters.

As one of Fredericton's few mixed-race couples, Hedley and Dorrit were "first" in many respects. In the Fredericton of the 1940s, anywhere they went, they made an entrance: the white, Austrian-Jewish Holocaust survivor married to the Black-Malecite Protestant from Lakeville Corner. With her thick accent, Dorrit was often perceived to be German, and to her that was akin to an insult. She never felt accepted by the local Jewish community because of her marriage to Hedley. She went to Passover ceremonies, but that was the extent of her religious observations. And even though she attended a couple of war bride functions in the early years, she had little in common with the mainly Christian, British wives in the city. Fortunately, there was one place where Dorrit always felt welcome: in the large and rambunctious Nash family. They accepted her without question.

After everything she had been through in Austria and Britain, Dorrit learned to stand up for herself. Not long after they moved into the little house Hedley built on Fredericton's north side, Dorrit walked across the street and introduced herself to the white next-door neighbour, Alice Thurnheer. "Hello," she said. "I'm Dorrit Nash, and I don't like prejudiced people." "Me neither!" replied Alice. The two women became friends for life.

After their children left the nest, Dorrit and Hedley started travelling. They visited their eldest daughter, Diane, in the Bahamas, and middle daughter, Denise, in Montreal en route. Deby also moved to Nassau in the late 1980s, so there was always a reason to plan a winter cruise. After Hedley passed away in 2000, Dorrit continued travelling and expanding her circle of friends. That changed in the summer of 2007, when she was felled by an aggressive hospital infection. She died suddenly on Friday, September 7, 2007.

Despite her cool relationship with the local Jewish community, Dorrit had always told her children that she wanted to be buried next to her mother, Irma, in Fredericton's Jewish cemetery. It is impossible to miss Irma Hacker's gravestone: engraved on the front are the words "VICTIM OF NAZI PERSECUTION" — one of only two markers in the graveyard that make a direct link to the ravages of the Holocaust. However, due to Orthodox tradition, the local rabbi refused to allow Dorrit's body to be buried next to her mother in the cemetery. In life, Dorrit's country and her family had been taken from her. It would not be so in death. Her daughters, as resilient and strong willed as Dorrit herself, went to the cemetery and scattered Dorrit's ashes over her mother's grave. Then they wrote the rabbi and told him that Dorrit was finally reunited with her people and her mother, forever.

While the focus of attention is typically on British and European war brides, New Brunswick servicemen also married women they met in other countries where they served during the war, including Bermuda and Newfoundland. Gloria (Hassel) Peters came from Spanish Point in beautiful, sunny Bermuda to Saint Paul, Kent County, a small settlement near Moncton. Further north, Annie (Gooseney) Hickie of St. John's, Newfoundland, was sixteen years old when she met her husband, Bill, who was from Jacquet River, NB. Bill was with the Royal Rifles of Canada, and the couple knew each other only three months before they married, on Bill's birthday, August 14, 1941. Two weeks later, Bill shipped out — the destination a secret, but since the men were issued summer clothing, rumour was they were going to Bermuda. By November, Annie knew that Bill was in Hong Kong. The Japanese attacked the colony on December 7, and after an eighteen-day battle, on Christmas Day, he and hundreds of Canadian defenders were taken prisoners of war. Annie never heard a word from him until the fall of Japan, on August 14, 1945 — their fourth wedding anniversary. Bill spent three months recuperating, and they were reunited in October 1945. His wages had accrued while he was a POW, and Annie had saved $40 a month from her spousal allowance, so with his re-establishment credits they were able to buy a small house in Saint John.

Bill worked as an orderly at the provincial hospital for the mentally ill, which was a tough job for a man who had survived a Japanese prison camp. He never spoke much about his experiences as a POW. Annie said "he suffered in silence," which was common for the men who had endured years of torture, deprivation, and arbitrary violence in the Japanese camps. Bill died in 2002, and Annie continued living in their home in Quispamsis.

It is generally assumed that all war brides came to Canada, but a small number of New Brunswick women married British, Australian, and even Norwegian men in the province during the Second World War, and moved away. Anna Hennessy was working at the Woodlands division of Bathurst Pulp and Paper in Bathurst when she met Captain Henrik Wesenberg, a Norwegian who had been at sea with his ship, the SS *Borgholm*, when the Nazis invaded Norway in April 1940. Henrik was in Bathurst, picking up a load of lumber, when he fell on deck and broke his wrist. Anna's sister, Lucy, worked for the only doctor in town, and she introduced them to each other. Henrik took part in the evacuation of Dunkirk, received a letter of citation for heroism while under German attack in the Humber River, took a German officer prisoner, and did convoy duty carrying weapons and ammunition to Britain and the Mediterranean during the war — all as a member of Norway's merchant navy.

Henrik and Anna married in Bathurst in 1946 and moved to Oslo, Norway, where they started a family. But talk of a cold war and fear of another invasion — this time by Russians — brought them back to Bathurst in the mid-1950s. They had six children, all of whom have visited their father's family in Oslo. Henrik died in 1974, and Anna took his ashes back to Norway to be buried.

Ruth Harris of Chatham was one of about four thousand Canadian women to fall in love with allied servicemen who were training in Canada with the British Commonwealth Air Training Plan. Ruth married Royal Australian Air Force officer Quentin Douglas Toppin in February 1943, and journeyed to Sydney, Australia, in 1944. A story about her, titled "Canadian Brides Are Welcomed to Australia," appeared in the *Telegraph-Journal* on November 21, 1946. In what seems to be a

Captain Henrik Wesenberg, Anna Hennessy, Lucy Hennessy, and Eileen Hennessy pose for a photo in the backyard of the Hennessy family homestead in Bathurst. Henrik, a member of the Norwegian merchant navy, happened to meet Anna when he was in port picking up a load of lumber. After the war, he and Anna married. They lived in Norway for six years and returned to Canada in the early 1950s. Courtesy of Lucy Jarratt

familiar pattern of war brides news coverage around the world, the article described how Ruth and several other Canadian women were settling in to their new lives down under. "Life here is very much like it is at home — except warmer," said one of the women, when asked how she liked Australia. "The people are friendly and genuine and seem sympathetic to the problems that may crop up for War Brides from overseas." And in a universal piece of advice that applies to any woman, at any time in the history of wartime love and marriage, she added: "You get adjusted to a new country just that much faster if you work on it."

Immigration Branch RG76 Vol 462 File 705870 Pt. 10

DEPARTMENT OF VETERANS' AFFAIRS October 1st, 1947

THE ADVISORY COMMITTEE ON VETERANS' DEPENDENTS OVERSEAS

ADDRESSES

———————, ——————   ——————————, N.B.

DEPENDENTS: Mrs Jane B. ——————,   c/o Aberdeen Royal Mental Hosp.
aged 40   1, Albyn Place, Aberdeen.
Child - ———— - aged 4   c/o Mrs. ————
                                     ——————————
                                     ————, Aberdeenshire.

SOCIAL SITUATION:

Married July 11/42. Veteran arranged wife's admission to above Institution on April 3/44 following child-birth. ———— was then placed on boarding basis with ————. ———— refuses to co-operate in sending ———— to Canada. Veteran wants wife and child to go forward together. Mr. Sheppard, Legal Officer, is dealing with case as it may involve legal action.

ILLNESS: Dr. Jeffs' Statement:- 17 Sep 47

Onset: January 1944   Diagnosis: Insane

Probable duration: Permanent   Last Medical Report - 3/4/47

COST: Parish rate £112.10.0 per year paid by Public Assistance authorities less payments from D.V.A.

SETTLEMENT ARRANGEMENTS:

Has completed a new house. His mother lives with him. He claims he could look after wife and child. Settlement arrangements for child are approved by Immigration Branch. Reasonably well established in an ———— business. Admission and care in Provincial Institution would be necessary, and Dr. Menzies Superintendent agreed to write to Dr. Jeffs.

AMOUNT TO PAY:

$51.12 - $37.20 to hospital, $13.92 to ————.

Ref. Nos   Immigration   ————

            National Health and Welfare: ————

Canadian Agency interested - Provincial Child welfare.

The Wives Bureau went to great lengths to reunite families torn apart by the war. In this case, a New Brunswick soldier was trying to have his wife and daughter brought to Canada, even though his wife had been certified "insane" and his daughter's caregiver in Scotland refused to cooperate with the authorities by letting the child leave for Canada. LAC RG76

Chapter Five

The Darker Side

Not all war brides who married Canadian servicemen came to this country. By the end of November 1946, there were still an estimated seven thousand women and children who had not formalized arrangements for their trip. Many wives simply refused to make the journey. Others failed to meet the standard for immigration and were refused entry by Canadian officials. How many of these women were married to New Brunswick servicemen is unknown, but it would not be an exaggeration to say there were hundreds. Other marriages simply ended badly or were endured — often under dreadful circumstances — for a lifetime.

As far as the Wives Bureau was concerned, you needed a very good excuse to refuse a free trip to Canada, and illness was one of them. One woman, who married an Acadian man serving with the Forestry Corps in Scotland, was diagnosed as insane and institutionalized at the Aberdeen Royal Mental Hospital following the birth of their daughter in April 1944. After the father returned to New Brunswick, the infant was fostered in Duncelt, Aberdeenshire, and, having grown attached to the child, the foster mother refused to allow the girl to leave for Canada. According to the bureau files, the husband considered legal action. He had built a house and started a business, and the settlement arrangements were deemed "Satisfactory" by the Immigration Branch. He wanted his wife and child to come to New Brunswick and, if necessary, his wife to

List F.
Miscellaneous.

List 6.
Sheet 1.

CONTINENTAL CASES

REGT'L. NO.	RANK	SURNAME	INITIALS	WIFE'S CHRISTIAN NAMES	IML/FILE REF.	REMARKS	COUNTRY
▬▬▬	Spr	▬▬▬	G.	Denise	▬▬▬	No Appin - awaiting medical.	France
▬▬▬	Pte	▬▬▬	L.J.	Alida J.	▬▬▬	Awaiting marriage cert. & Med:	Holland
▬▬▬	Pte	▬▬▬	P.G.	Dirkje	▬▬▬	Wife imprisoned.	Holland
▬▬▬	Pte	▬▬▬	A.	Pieternella	▬▬▬	Awaiting child's Med:	Holland
▬▬▬	Dvr	▬▬▬	E.O.	Marie K.	▬▬▬	Awaiting Med:	Denmark
▬▬▬	Tpr	▬▬▬	H.F.	Beit L.	▬▬▬	Marriage not valid	Holland
▬▬▬	Pte	▬▬▬	H.J.	Cecile	▬▬▬	Awaiting medical	Belgium
▬▬▬	Pte	▬▬▬	L.T.	Magdalena	▬▬▬	Awaiting medical	Holland
▬▬▬	Pte	▬▬▬	B.E.	Justina	▬▬▬	Awaiting medical	Belgium
▬▬▬	Pte	▬▬▬	R.A.	Roelofje	▬▬▬	Interview re separation	Holland
▬▬▬	Pte	▬▬▬	W.J.	3 children only.	▬▬▬	Mother in CCIm, Appin later.	Hungary
▬▬▬	Gnr	▬▬▬	O.F.	Maria L.	▬▬▬	Awaiting child's Med:	Italy
▬▬▬	Pte	▬▬▬	R.W.	Jacoba A.	▬▬▬	Awaiting interview with wife.	Holland
▬▬▬	Cpl	▬▬▬	H.R.	Francisca	▬▬▬	Marriage not valid	Holland
▬▬▬	CSM	▬▬▬	O.F.	Christina	▬▬▬	Wife obtaining divorce	Holland
▬▬▬	LAC	▬▬▬	V.H.	Lydia L.S.I.G.	▬▬▬	Case being re-opened	Belgium
▬▬▬ (RCAF)	L/Cpl	▬▬▬	M.G.	Marie		Wife unable to be contacted	Holland
D.158781	Sgt	▬▬▬	R.	Greda P.	▬▬▬	Awaiting birth cert. Med:	Holland

As the Canadian Wives Bureau tried to wind up operations in Britain and Europe, it compiled lists of "problem cases" where wives refused to come to Canada due to marital estrangement or for health reasons such as pregnancy or illness. At the other end of the scale were husbands who refused to accept their wives in Canada, and cases where the Immigration Branch refused to allow wives transportation because their settlement arrangements were unsatisfactory. LAC RG24 be admitted to the provincial hospital. By October 1947, the case was still unresolved, and there is no record of what happened to the child.

Another good reason not to travel to Canada was the death of a parent. Mrs. Catherine (Baker) MacKinnon of Urmston, Lancashire, delayed her journey until January 1947 because her father was dying. She waited until he passed away before completing her travel arrangements with the Wives Bureau. The bureau actually closed operations that same month, handing over all its files to the Immigration Branch. Included in the boxes of transferred material were about twenty sheets of names, listing the reasons those women weren't coming to Canada. One man from New Brunswick had "VDS" (venereal disease symptoms) and he did not want his wife to proceed, even though she wanted to come. Another man could not be found and was believed to be living with a common-law wife. Yet another was in jail, and one man had committed suicide. But for the majority, the reasons for not travelling to Canada were "marital estrangement" and "divorce pending."

The stories behind these failed marriages must have been heartbreaking, but in some ways, these women were lucky: they found out before they came to Canada that their lives here would not be a fairy tale. As more women started arriving in the province, in 1944 and 1945, the issue of what to do with wives whose marriages had fallen apart was raised in the House of Commons. On April 10, 1945, the lot of British war brides "deserted in Canada" was raised by Colonel A.J. Brooks (PC-Royal), who told of a case in Woodstock, NB, that had been brought to the attention of the Red Cross. Afraid of setting a precedent, the society wanted to know where the wife should turn for financial assistance and advice. "The government may say that these are cases which must be dealt with by the civilian authorities," Colonel Brooks observed, "but it should be remembered that the civilian authorities in the smaller towns, except through charitable organizations, are not in a position to help these people."

Colonel Brooks was absolutely right. In New Brunswick, social services as we know them today were virtually non-existent, the people who worked in the field were well-intentioned but untrained, and there was little in the form of any follow-up referred to by the army. A Department of National Defence analysis of social services in Canada in 1947 showed "many weaknesses" in New Brunswick. More than in any other province, women who ended up in problem marriages here had nobody to turn to and nowhere to go for help. Having brought these women over to Canada on a "one-way passage," the army was reluctant to get involved in their marital problems. DND turned to the Department of Veterans Affairs for guidance. But DVA washed its hands of the issue, passing the buck on to provincial social service agencies and charitable organizations. The last hope was the Red Cross, a society that was ill-equipped to assist even Canadian-born women facing the same problems of abuse and desertion.

In the final analysis, war brides in Canada were citizens and, like other Canadian women, they could expect no special treatment when they needed help. In the days before welfare and domestic violence programs, they were largely on their own — without their own families to turn to for support and guidance. There are some terrible stories of war brides whose lives in New Brunswick were characterized by years of physical and emotional abuse, whose husbands terrorized the children with threats and beatings, and whose dreams were shattered almost from the minute they arrived in the province. Whether the rate of abuse in these marriages was higher than the provincial average has never been determined. However, we do know anecdotally that abuse rates appear to have been higher in marriages where the husband was a combat veteran suffering from what we now call operational stress injuries. One thing the wives in these troubled marriages had in common was the complete absence of help from all levels of government.

The first sign that something could go wrong was the designation "Settlement Arrangements Unsatisfactory" in a war bride's file overseas. Unsatisfactory arrangements meant that Immigration officials had decided the destination to which the woman was headed was not suitable and therefore refused to grant her permission to come to Canada until better arrangements could be found. Up until November 1946, the Wives Bureau stuck to its guns about the entire issue of satisfactory or unsatisfactory settlement arrangements. Thousands of wives and children had to wait until better accommodations could be found before they were brought to Canada. But as pressure increased on the Wives Bureau to wind down its affairs before January 1947, it appears that the bureau's commitment to ensuring satisfactory arrangements for Canada's newest citizens began to waver. In its rush to fill the last war bride ships with these stragglers, the Wives Bureau loosened the requirements, and into this fold were drawn many unsuspecting women who probably should not have come to Canada.

The late Mrs. Sally White (a pseudonym), who arrived in Halifax on the *Aquitania* on February 5, 1947, was one of these unfortunate war brides. She was headed to a small town in southern New Brunswick to be reunited with her husband Bill (a pseudonym), whom she had married in April 1946. Sally had filled out all the forms and gone through all the examinations, but she was reluctant to come to Canada, perhaps sensing that the rushed marriage to her Canadian soldier may have been a mistake. She delayed as long as she could, but in January 1947, she boarded the *Aquitania* in Southampton with nine hundred other latecomers and made her way to Canada. Sally thought she was coming to a better life in New Brunswick and had every reason to believe so: didn't Immigration tell her that the settlement arrangements in Canada were satisfactory? But at this end, the system was falling apart.

When shown the Wives Bureau documents a few years ago, Sally's youngest daughter, Colleen (a pseudonym), remembered her mother saying that the Immigration people had not checked out the place that she was coming to. Normal practice would have included a home visit and interviews with the people living there. Instead, they wrote Bill, and he wrote back to assure them that everything was fine. From such an investigation came the stamp of approval "Settlement Arrangements Satisfactory" and Sally's permission to come to Canada.

If Sally had only known what lay ahead, she would never have boarded that ship. After a brief reunion in Halifax, Bill and Sally drove to New Brunswick, where Bill promptly announced to his shocked wife that he was going to introduce her to his five children!

The Darker Side | 107

Sally had had no idea that Bill had ever been married, let alone that he was the father of five children. According to family lore, Bill had been married before the war, and when he joined up in 1939, his first wife turned to prostitution for survival. The children were taken away and fostered out for the war's duration. When Sally arrived, the first thing Bill did was go to his thirteen-year-old son's school, haul him out of class, and introduce the child to his "new mother." The same thing was done for the four other children.

Twenty-four-year-old Sally, fresh from England and full of hopes and dreams for a new life in Canada, soon found herself the stepmother of five very unhappy children, who made it abundantly clear that they did not want to be uprooted from the foster homes where they had been living happily for the past six years. Bill got his way, however, and the children were taken out of foster care. Before long Sally was pregnant with the first of eight children, and Bill began to show his true colours. An alcoholic brute who abused his wife and children, Bill threatened to kill them all on more than one occasion. His daughter recalls one incident where he came home in a drunken stupor and chased the children down the road with a shotgun. When Sally was nine months pregnant with twins, he kicked her in the stomach, and she went into premature labour. Beloved pets were shot in front of the children. Colleen said, "It was best not to love anything in that house."

Such memories die hard. The entire family was affected emotionally by Bill's cruelty. It was only after his death, and then Sally's many years later, that the thirteen siblings were able to close the wounds of their tortured childhood. Was Bill's behaviour the result of his wartime service, or would he have been a violent abuser in any case? While PTSD is widely accepted today as a serious mental illness afflicting soldiers who have experienced the horrors of war, at the end of the Second World War it certainly was not.

Barbara Jones (a pseudonym) was another war bride who was fairly certain her husband suffered from PTSD and felt it partially explained why he treated her so badly, especially in the early years. George (a pseudonym) was a good-looking and jovial twenty-two-year-old when

Barbara met him in southern England. They married about six months later and were very much in love. When she became pregnant with her first child, George was sent off for training in advance of the Italian invasion, and she recalled how concerned he was, phoning every chance he could and telling her how much he missed and loved her.

Then came Italy and later the campaign in Holland: eighteen months on the front lines in an infantry battalion. When they met again, in May 1945, George was a complete stranger. "He wasn't the same man I married," she said. Standing in front of her was a nerve-wracked shell, whose Military Cross could not stave off the horrors he had witnessed at the front. When George first came back to New Brunswick, he spent most of his time drinking himself into a stupor at the Legion and getting into fist fights with his war buddies — to whom he then had to apologize the next day. He was kicked out of the Legion and told not to come back, but he managed to talk his way back in with a promise to behave.

George was never able to hold down a full-time job, so Barbara had to work to support the family. He suffered terrible nightmares, shouting out and kicking his legs in bed. He went to the DVA psychiatrist in Saint John for help, in the late 1940s and early 1950s, but all the doctor did was prescribe increasingly large doses of medication for his nerves. As Barbara said, "all they did was drug him up," and combined with the alcohol abuse, he was incoherent most of the time. About ten years after the war, Barbara accompanied George to Saint John, fully intending to have a serious talk with the psychiatrist about all the prescription medication he was giving her husband. At the last minute, George would not let her into the doctor's office, so she never did get to talk to the man. Not long after, the DVA psychiatrist committed suicide, and things went from bad to worse; but Barbara stayed. There was nowhere else to go. Assaulting your wife was not a crime in the 1940s, and would not be for nearly thirty years. Transition houses were unheard of, and the social expectations of married women ruled out returning home to Britain or Europe as a divorcée as an option.

Of course, not every woman who abandoned New Brunswick and her soldier husband to return to Britain or Europe was the victim of abuse.

40 War Brides Return To U. K.

BOSTON, June 27 — (A. P.) — About 40 British and French war wives, their romantic marriages to Canadian and Newfoundland soldiers shattered, were homeward bound on the Ile de France today.

The wives, several of whom had babies, arrived here Tuesday from Halifax. They said the arduous life in the Canadian woods and in Nova Scotia and Newfoundland was the cause of the broken marriages.

"We didn't know what we were getting into," one wife said. "We'd never get use to that kind of life. We just had to call it quits and go back home."

Nearly all the wives took advantage of a ruling allowing them to take from this country $50 worth of foodstuff and $25 worth of fabrics.

Articles, like this one, which appeared in Canadian newspapers in 1947 raised concerns that war brides were not faring well in their wartime marriages. We will never know how many women returned to Britain and Europe from Canada, but they were in the minority. When faced with adversity, most war brides refused to give up. They dug in their heels and made good, loving homes for their husbands and families. *Telegraph-Journal,* 28 June, 1947, p. 7

As the newspapers of the period show, many women just could not settle into this completely different way of life. An article in the *Telegraph-Journal* on June 28, 1947, titled "40 War Brides Return to UK," quoted one woman as saying, "We didn't know what we were getting into. We'd never get used to that kind of life. We just had to call it quits and go back home."

Sandra Paine's mother stayed fourteen months in Tabusintac, near Bathurst, before she went back to England with her two children. It took nearly thirty years before Sandra met her father again, and she was so impressed by him, the people, and the province that she and her husband immigrated to New Brunswick. Sandra's mother, Marjorie Wariner, was from Polegate, England. Marjorie was an only child whom Sandra describes as "spoiled." Marjorie met Willard Murray of Tabusintac at the Merry Tadpole, a pub and dance hall in Polegate. Willard was with the 28th Field Battery (Newcastle) of the 2nd Field Regiment, RCA, and had been in England since September 1939. They married in 1943, and Sandra was born in 1944. After the war, Willard was repatriated to Canada, and eight months later, Marjorie and Sandra arrived in New Brunswick.

Tabusintac, in 1946, was radically different from what Marjorie had left behind in England. "Before the year was out, I believe Mum was repenting at leisure," said Sandra. "With the arrival of winter she had totally given in. She took to her room and stayed there reading most of the time." Another child, a boy, was born in March, but by this time Marjorie's nerves were beginning to suffer, and she became more unhappy as the days went by. She could not adapt to Tabusintac and wrote home, begging her father to send her money for a ticket. Being a softhearted man, he could not refuse his only daughter. In early June 1947, Marjorie and the two children sailed from Halifax, back to England after fourteen months in New Brunswick.

Over the years, Sandra lost touch with her father, but she always knew where he lived. In 1977, she connected with him again, and the first thing he did was invite her to come and visit. When Sandra told her mother she was going to Canada, Marjorie was not impressed. "What the bloody hell do you want to go there for?" Marjorie demanded. But it was Sandra's life, and her father, so she and her husband, Roger, flew to New Brunswick and were overwhelmed by their reception. Three years later they immigrated to Canada, and settled in New Brunswick.

Sandra's father died of cancer in October 1982. On his last day, he asked to speak to her alone. "His request was for me to make sure that nobody put the Maple Leaf flag on his coffin," Sandra recalled. "As a soldier, he served and fought under the Union Jack; this was his last battle, and that was his flag of choice. I didn't have to worry, the Legion made sure of it. Willard Peck Murray, my dear father, finally gave in on October 28, 1982, and so ended another chapter of my life."

Sandra and her father had only a few short years together, but other children of Canadian servicemen never met their fathers at all. During the war years, an estimated twenty-three thousand "war babies" were born out of wedlock from liaisons between Canadian servicemen and British women. Typically these children were given up for adoption or, if they were lucky, were raised by grandparents and other relatives as their own. That's what happened to world-famous blues guitarist, Eric Clapton. Born in his grandparents' home in Ripley, Surrey, to sixteen-

Patricia Clapton MacDonald (right) at a get-together with other military wives and husbands in her backyard in Oromocto, in the 1970s.

Courtesy of Gordon Hovey

year-old Patricia "Pat" Clapton, Eric never knew his father, Edward Fryer, a Canadian soldier from Montreal.

After Eric was born, Pat married a Canadian named Frank MacDonald, from Lower Glencoe, Nova Scotia, and in December 1946, she came to Canada on the war bride ship *Samaria*. In the 1970s, Pat and Frank MacDonald lived in Oromocto where Frank continued his military career, eventually rising to the rank of regimental sergeant major (RSM). They had three children, Brian, Heather, and Cheryl.

In the summer of 1974, twenty-six-year-old Brian was killed in a motorcycle accident in Summerside, Prince Edward Island, where he was serving with the Canadian Forces. Although Eric hadn't seen much of his brother since they were teenagers and they were, as Eric wrote in his autobiography, "hardly close," the news still saddened him because he "liked him a lot." Clapton, along with his girlfriend, Pattie Boyd — famous herself for her earlier marriage to George Harrison of the Beatles — came to Canada to attend the funeral. Also present was Rose Clapp, Eric's grandmother, who had raised him in England after Pat married Frank and came to Canada.

Eric's sister, Heather, who was just a teenager herself, invited her boyfriend and his cousin over to the house to meet Eric. Both boys had heard Heather talk about Clapton, but this was the first time they had met the musician. They spent about an hour at the house, had a drink, and listened while Clapton talked about Brian and shed a tear or two. On the wall were a number of his gold albums and framed records, including "I Shot The Sheriff."

An eighteen-year-old student, working that summer as RSM MacDonald's personal assistant, also met Eric Clapton during that weekend in Oromocto. He recalled MacDonald saying that he knew the Beatles and other famous rock stars, but hadn't really believed it was true, until the Saturday morning he was summoned to the MacDonald home on an "emergency." When he walked into the living room he got the shock of his life to see Eric Clapton and Pattie Boyd. After brief introductions, he was asked to drive the MacDonald family to the funeral in PEI, closely followed by a limousine carrying the guitarist and his girlfriend. The service was held that afternoon in Summerside, and that evening, they held a wake of sorts in the Brothers Two, a restaurant and bar: there the mourners were treated to an impromptu performance by none other than Eric Clapton.

Ron Gourlay was also born out of wedlock, but he lived with his mother, Winnifred Gashen, a divorcée from Scotland who struck out on her own in London, after Ron was born. If it hadn't been for a German bombing raid in 1942, Ron might have lived a comfortable life with her in Britain. Instead, in April 1946, he ended up in New Brunswick with his mother and her new husband.

The memory of that bombing raid in 1942 was seared in Ron's memory for more than one reason. His mother was trapped under debris following the raid, and a passing soldier, called to assist in the rescue, dug Ron's mother out. The soldier was Rifleman William Harrington of the Regina Rifles, who was from Hayden Ridge, near Juniper, New Brunswick. He saved Winnifred's life, and the couple fell in love. The following year, they were married, and Ron's destiny in Canada was forged.

Ron was just seven years old when he came to Canada, but it was clear from the start that his stepfather didn't want the boy around. When Winnifred and William had a baby in 1947, there was no room in the family for Ron. By age eleven, he was out of the house completely and boarding at a private home close to the rural school in Juniper. He never lived with his mother again. When he was in grade nine, Ron was offered a job making good money, so he dropped out of school and started working in the woods, then joined the Canadian army in 1956. When he was a young man, he went back to Scotland to meet his mother's family. There was only an elderly aunt left, and she was not very welcoming.

Ron didn't blame his mother for the way things turned out in Canada. He knew she was just as much a victim of circumstances as was he. Ron had a successful career in the military and had his own share of stories to tell about the conflicts he'd been involved with: he served in Vietnam, was taken prisoner, was tortured, and escaped; but he always went back in memory to that night in 1942 and a bombing raid that changed his life forever.

~

We will never know how many war brides returned to Britain or Europe when their marriages faltered in New Brunswick. Once they landed in Canada, war brides became Canadian citizens; and when they decided to go back, they were no longer classified as "war brides." They simply joined the exodus of outbound passengers on ships or planes destined for the other side of the Atlantic.

Among their contemporaries, it seems that everyone knew at least one war bride who gave up and went back home to the comfort of her family and friends. No one could blame a woman for leaving when the "ranch" she was promised by her husband, overseas, turned out to be a tarpaper shack along the side of the road, or when she found out, too late, that the war had permanently changed the man she married. "He wasn't the same anymore" was an oft-heard phrase, and it had a devastating effect on some marriages.

There have been plenty of disappointments and tears shed, down through the generations, over wartime love that was lost in Canada. For some war brides, the sparkle quickly wore off when they came face to face with the reality of everyday life in New Brunswick; the rough life on rural farms, homesickness, and cultural differences were a fact that cannot be denied. So, too, were the stories of violence, abuse, and neglect at the hands of a husband and father. As we can see, some women left while others stayed. It was a different time then, and whether one choice was better than the other is in the eye of the beholder.

One woman, whose life in New Brunswick didn't turn out as she had hoped, when asked if she would do it again, said this:

> That's a big question. We live our lives as they unfold, and things aren't laid out in a certain pattern. We go which way they turn. Who is to say, if we had gone another way, if things would have turned out better or worse?

> St. Stephen
>
> Dear Mrs Smith,
>
> The members of the St Croix Chapter Imperial Order, Daughters of the Empire are giving a tea, in honor of overseas brides in this community at 3 o'clock, December the second, in the Rotary rooms (over Hyslop's store). We are looking forward to having you with us.
>
> Please reply to the Regent, Mrs. Roy Hill — St Stephen.
>
> Your children will be welcome.

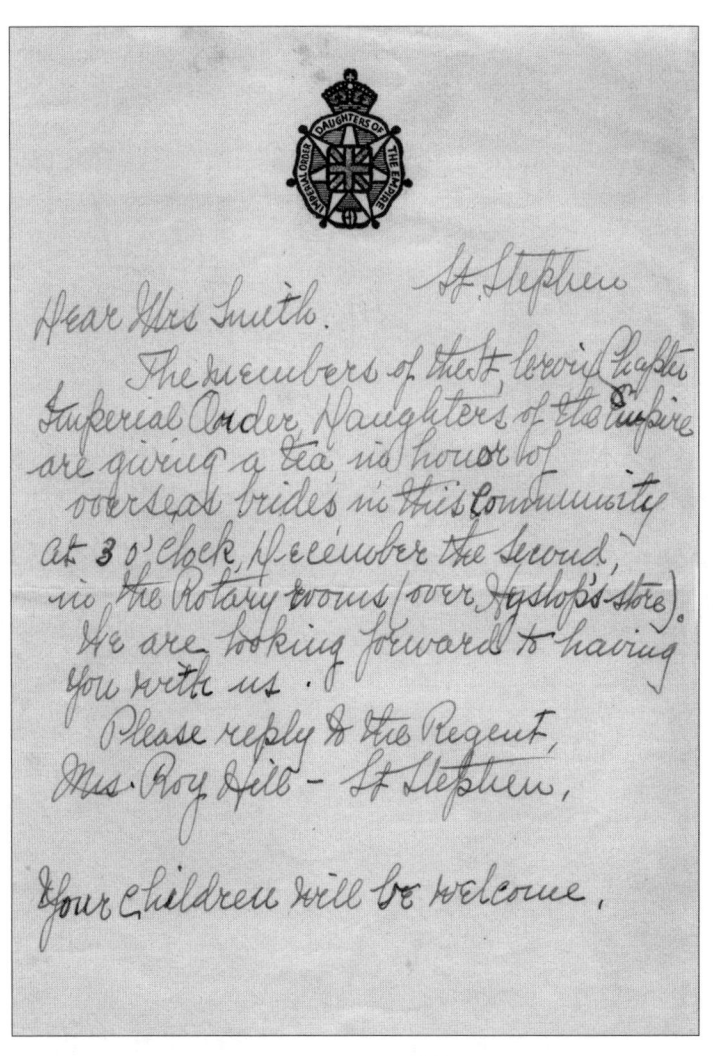

Local women's organizations like the IODE made a concerted effort to welcome overseas wives into their communities. In this handwritten invitation, the St. Croix IODE cordially invited Mrs. Selma Smith to a tea in honour of war brides, to be held at the Rotary Club, above the Hyslop Store. Note the reference to children: "Your children will be welcome." Courtesy of Rose Burke

Conclusion

For the first two years after the war brides arrived in New Brunswick, there was an intense interest in their well-being. Local women's groups like the Imperial Order of Daughters of the Empire (IODE), Women's Institute, and Red Cross went out of their way to welcome these new immigrants into their communities. All over the province, society ladies rolled out the red carpet, hosting teas, parties, wedding and baby showers. Dutch war bride Selma (Kater) Smith of Upper Mills kept her handwritten invitation to a December 2, 1946, "tea in honour of overseas war brides" that was organized by the St. Croix chapter of the IODE. "We are looking forward to having you with us," the invitation said — and most importantly, for a new mother like Selma, "Your children are welcome."

In the Social Section of the *Telegraph-Journal* and *Daily Gleaner*, numerous articles appeared about events held across the province to honour war brides. Some were large gatherings, with twenty or more wives in attendance. In Saint John, the YMCA organized a large group of war brides who met regularly until the late 1940s. At Christmas 1947, the Temperance Society held a big party, complete with Santa Claus and presents: a group photograph shows more than fifty women with their children, mostly infants and toddlers. In Fredericton, the Red Cross did the same, holding meetings at the Royal Canadian Legion. Other events were small, private affairs, like the "cup and saucer shower" that was

The Saint John Temperance Society was one of many organizations that went out of its way to help war brides and their children celebrate Christmas in 1946. Similar events occurred across the province, hosted by a variety of service organizations including the Red Cross and YMCA.

Courtesy of Jean Belding

held at the home of Mr. and Mrs. I.K. Titus, on May 1, 1946, for Scottish war bride Mrs. A. Kennedy McKnight of Sussex.

The ties that bound these women together weakened over the years. In cities and villages around New Brunswick, weekly meetings shifted to monthly and then to perhaps once a year. As the years passed, interest in the war brides faded, and most of the groups folded. It should come as no surprise that, with families growing, children going to school, and, in many cases, mothers working, there simply wasn't enough time in a busy woman's day to attend war bride club meetings. Besides, they were settling in, developing their own circles of friends, and becoming more Canadian with each passing year. They were no longer the lovestruck

Plaster Rock war brides gather for a reunion in 1986. Seated among them are two war brides from the First World War. <small>Courtesy of Doris Lloyd</small>

young brides they had been a few years before. And in the midst of a post-war baby boom, many women had very large families. It was not unusual for war brides to have as many as ten or more children, like Vera (Dauncey) Ruff of Plaster Rock, who had eleven.

As their children grew up, war brides became involved in their communities and schools, taking leadership roles in local voluntary organizations such as the Boy Scouts and Girl Guides, the Home and School Association, and library boards. Later, as the children left the nest, some women became involved in local politics; Dorothy (Currie) Hyslop of St. Stephen served ten years as Village Councillor and was chairperson of the school board; Elsie (Spinner) Nadeau of Eel River Crossing was the first Village Clerk, and in 2005, she was Dalhousie's Citizen of the Year. Barbara (Andrews) Huard of Bathurst was the first female president of the Herman J. Good VC Royal Canadian Legion, becoming one of the very few women to head the traditionally male-dominated organization.

In the mid-1970s, a resurgence of interest in the war bride story coincided with the publication of Joyce Hibbert's book, *The War Brides*. Hibbert was the first to tell their stories, both the good and the bad, and it attracted considerable interest across Canada. At the same time, a group of women in Saskatchewan, headed by British war bride Gloria Brock,

Conclusion | 119

established the Saskatchewan War Brides Association (SWBA). Its annual reunions were a magnet for women across Canada who were eager to get together again after so many years.

Motivated by the success of the Saskatchewan association, war bride groups started organizing on a provincial level across Canada, and by the late 1980s, there were formal and informal groups meeting on a regular basis in nearly every province. English war bride Doris (Field) Lloyd of Plaster Rock attended a reunion in England, in 1986, where she met some women from Saskatchewan. When she returned to Canada, she decided it was time to establish a formal organization in New Brunswick. In 1989, Doris did all the legwork involved in founding the association. She brought together a board of like-minded women in Plaster Rock and had a constitution and bylaws drawn up, and the New Brunswick War Brides Association (NBWBA) was born.

Nearly twenty years later, the NBWBA still meets annually for reunions in Fredericton. When New Brunswick became the first province in Canada to declare 2006 Year of the War Bride, it renewed interest in the war brides' place in Canadian history. Dozens of events were held in small and large communities throughout the province, and a pilgrimage back to Pier 21 attracted international attention. Across Canada, six other provinces followed suit, and the ensuing media coverage brought many war brides out of their rural settings for the first time since they arrived in Canada.

The reality is, however, that their numbers are now dwindling quickly in every province; most war brides are in their mid-eighties, their husbands are gone, and they are not as agile as they would prefer to be. Canes and walkers are common at the reunions, and none can do the jig or the Lambeth Walk like she used to. But the original vision of a social club created by and for New Brunswick war brides still lives on, and as long as there is a will and a way to keep meeting once a year, the organization will continue to exist.

Time will tell when the last reunion of the NBWBA is held and the group retires its charter. Even if the organization does fold, there is a growing consensus among war bride children and grandchildren that now, more than ever, it is important to record the histories of their mothers and grandmothers who came to New Brunswick for the love of a Canadian serviceman. In so doing, they can help to preserve a disappearing chapter of our military heritage that is, without any doubt, one of the most fascinating and romantic of the Second World War.

Acknowledgements

I would like to acknowledge the following persons for their help and assistance in making this book a reality. First of all, many thanks are owed to Marc Milner and Brent Wilson of the Gregg Center for the Study of War and Society, who first approached me to write a volume in the New Brunswick Military Heritage Book Series. Their recognition of the war bride story as part of our military history is a validation of all my work for the past twenty years.

To my friends, Doris Lloyd and Zoe Boone, founding president and acting president of the New Brunswick War Brides Association, respectively, I owe so much; without their help and vast network of personal connections across the province and, indeed, across Canada, I would not have been able to develop such a broad outlook on the war bride story.

To my war bride friend, author Eswyn Lyster, I am indebted, for she is always there to help whenever I need clarification. Thank you, as well, to researcher/writer Annette Fulford, whose brief history of the New Brunswick war brides of the First World War appears as an appendix in this book. To researcher John Boers of LiberationChildren.org, thank you for lending your expertise in deciphering Second World War Canadian military personnel registration numbers. Thank you, Patsy Hennessy, for your unfailing support and assistance in obtaining wedding and birth certificates and passenger lists online. To Todd Spencer and Erin Baribeau, thank you for your hard work in the microfilm records. To Maryann and Christine Morgan, thank you for transcribing the wartime newspaper articles.

What follows is an alphabetical list of all the New Brunswick war brides, their children and grandchildren, and others with a connection to the war bride story, who shared their family histories, photographs, and archival documents. If I have forgotten to include anyone who so generously contributed to this book, please forgive me, for it was not intended.

Doris (Legate) Amos, Isabella (Brand) Anderson, Jean (Attwood) Belding, Edna (Darby) Blanchette, Gail Blanchette, Zoe (Blair) Boone, Rose (O'Reilly) Boulay, May (Armstrong) Brockway, Barbara Brosnan, Rose Burke, Joyce (Ward) Buzzell, Peter Buzzell, Rhoda Carrier, Allan Dickson, Cathie (Robertson) Elliot, Charles Ferris, Lynn Fitzgerald, Madeline (Rusbridge) Fitzgerald, Hilda (Smith) Fyffe, Cindy Gaffney, Barbara Goodwin, Ron Goulay, Annie (Hill) Grant, Elaine Grijm, Pam Hay, Annie (Gooseney) Hickie, Betty (Lowthian) Hillman, Barbara (Miles) Holmes, Gordon Hovey, Barbara (Andrews) Huard, Dorothy (Currie) Hyslop, Tim Jacques, Lucy (Hennessy) Jarratt, Hilda (Jones) Jenkins Jarvis, Winifred (Green) Keirstead, Nicole Lagacy, Anna (Perugine) and Aurele Lavigne, Joan (Hawtin) LeBlanc, Doris (Field) Lloyd, Iona and Joan Loosen, Mary (Ralston) MacKellar, Yvonne (French) Maillet, Doris (Farrow) Marks, Dot (Upton) Matchett, Rita (Scrase) Maunder, Brenda (Rudd) McArthur, Eileen (Meaden) and Bill Mesheau, Angela Michaud, Sam Mullin, Ruth Murgatroyd, May and Eileen (Goulding) Murray, Deby Nash, Donna Marie Noble, Maria (Egbars) Ouellette, Sandra and Roger Paine, Mary (Parr) Palmater, Mike Palmater, Irene Poirier, Sandra Pond, Barbara Priestly, Jeannette Rasmussen, Nan (King) Rioux, Kay (Douglass) Ruddick, Vera (Dauncey) Ruff, Winifred (Martin) Rutledge, Maureen Scott, Betty (Silk) Smith, Laverne Stewart, Fay Tidd, Alice (Rondeau) and Jim Tranquilla, Jim and Lisa Tranquilla, Russel Weller, Anna (Hennessy) Wesenberg, Delice (de-Wolf) Wilby, Joe Wilby, Susan Willis, Kathleen (Smith) Withers, Ruth Withers, Judy Woodside.

In memory of: the late Maria Zellie (Despontin) Burris, Betty (Sheppee) Campbell, Maud Blanche (Cornish) Carson, Johan (Hillis) DeWitt, Sylvia (Rusbridge) Dickson, Mabel (Cackett) Dunphy, Patricia (Marriott) Ferris, Ada (Cloke) Grant, Phyllis (Head) Grover, Winnifred (Gourlay) Harrington, Mary (Didlick) Imhoff, Anne (Biles) Johnston, Mona (Ogg) Loosen, Catherine (Baker) MacKinnon, Ethel "Queenie"

(Mitchell) Marney, Rose (Connoly) McLenaghan, Kate Elizabeth (Smith) Mullin, Elsie (Spinner) Nadeau, Dorris (Hacker) Nash, Jean (Keegan) Paul, Selma (Kater) Smith, Mildred (Young) Sowers, Edith (Dasch) Tompkins.

Finally, I'd like to thank my husband Dan Weston, without whose support I would never have been able to complete this volume.

Maud and William Carson on their wedding day, December 22, 1917. Both Maud and her husband died in the 1918 influenza epidemic in Holtville, NB, leaving behind an eight-day-old infant named James, who became the centre of a custody battle. James served overseas during the Second World War. Courtesy of Rhoda Carrier

Appendix

The War Brides of the First World War

Contributed by Annette Fulford

Canadian soldiers serving overseas during the First World War brought home nearly thirty-five thousand British and European war brides. How many women married New Brunswickers is unknown, but anecdotal evidence indicates there were at least a few hundred war brides in the province by 1920. These veterans' wives shared many of the same hardships as those who came to the province in the 1940s — but the war brides of the First World War dealt with some unique circumstances that would have challenged even the hardiest pioneer.

Many travelled during the influenza epidemic of 1918-19 and, although some were able to travel with their husbands, even sailing into the port of Saint John before and after the Halifax Explosion of 1917, for many the trip was nothing short of a nightmare. War brides and children crossed the Atlantic under adverse conditions, berthed in overcrowded, substandard accommodations, which, in at least one case, led to a public inquiry in Canada. Nor did their trials end once they were safely settled in their new homes. Families who prospered in the 1920s shared equally in the suffering caused by the Depression of the 1930s, and many war brides watched as their young sons headed off to another European war in 1939.

Ethel Marney travelled to the Dominion in 1918, while her husband William was still overseas. She sailed on the troopship *Northland*, which departed from Liverpool in December 1918. When the *Northland* docked at Halifax, many of the passengers complained bitterly to the press about the quality of the food and accommodations. At the inquest that followed, there were allegations that stewards held back food and sold it at black-market prices; soldiers complained about inadequate berthing arrangements and washing facilities.

Several ships that arrived at Saint John in January 1919 experienced similar conditions. Headlines read "Rats Drive Women Up on Decks" on the *Tunisian* and "*Scandinavian* Arrives After Trying Voyage — Influenza Breaks Out During Passage."

War brides arriving at Saint John were brought to an immigration shed consisting of a long reception room, a smaller room filled with beds for sick passengers, and a nursery and washroom, which had "unlimited supplies and medicines and everything a baby sick or well could possibly want." There was also a kitchen, which connected with the reception room where the YWCA and local Volunteer Aid Detachments (VADs) served the war brides "hot drinks, sandwiches, and cakes." The women were treated to a cup of tea and light meal in the rest area, and after they were processed through immigration, they were escorted to the train for the short trip to their final destinations in New Brunswick.

But safe arrival in Canada did not mean that tragedy had been averted, as the tale of Maud Cornish reveals. Born in 1895 at Bristol, Gloucestershire, she married William Carson of Holtville, Northumberland County, in December 1917. Maud was three months pregnant when she travelled to Canada with her new husband in April 1918. She gave birth to their only son on November 6, 1918; then the flu epidemic swept through the household and killed Maud, her husband, and her father-in-law. Only the eight-day-old baby and his elderly grandmother survived. A custody battle ensued between the neighbours — who took in the infant — and his aunt, Christina Plume. After seeking legal advice and with the help of the sheriff, Christina finally got custody of her nephew and raised him as one of her own.

Kate Smith was born in 1897 in Cheshunt, Hertfordshire, and met Private Samuel Mullin from Exmoor, Northumberland County, at a dance. They were married in 1919 at Camberwell, London. Kate travelled to Canada during the summer of 1919 on the troopship *Baltic*, arriving at Halifax on August 21, 1919. Sam found employment with the New Brunswick Telephone Company, and they moved around the province, living for a number of years in Woodstock, Saint John, and Campbellton. Sadly, the marriage broke up in 1935, after sixteen years, and Kate took her two Canadian-born children back to England. She died in England in December 2005 at the age of one hundred and eight.

Mabel Cackett was born in Ashford, Kent, in 1893. During the war, Mabel became pregnant by her fiancé, a French-Canadian pilot. He was killed in the air over France and she was left to face the disapproval of her parents. Then she met Peter Dunphy, a Canadian soldier from Prince Edward Island. Despite her parents' protests, Peter and Mabel were determined to marry, and one year after the birth of her child, they did just that. Mabel travelled alone to Canada, in December 1919, on the SS *Carmania,* intending to send for her child once she was settled. They moved to Saint John where Peter opened a bootmaker's shop. The couple had eight children together, but Mabel's parents would not allow her first child to join them in New Brunswick.

Ethel Violet Mitchell met William Marney of Pinder, NB, at a dance. William was with the 55th Battalion and had gone overseas in 1915. Ethel travelled to Canada in December 1918 but found it hard to settle. She was homesick "beyond measure" and desperately missed her family in England. In the late 1920s, she returned to her homeland to live for a few years with her two sons, Alden and Glenn. However, in 1932, she returned to Canada on the *Montcalm* and lived in New Brunswick until her death in 1962.

Maria Zellie Despontin was born in 1898 at Marche-les-dames, Belgium. It is not known when Maria met William Burris, but it was probably during the Canadian advance through Belgium in late 1918. They married in 1919, and Maria came to Canada with her husband on the *Metagama*, which arrived at Quebec on June 3, 1919. They lived in Dalhousie at first but then built a house nearby in Eel River Crossing. Maria's mother tongue was French, but her husband's family was English-speaking, so that is the language she used after her children were born. Later, when the children were older, she opened her own clothing store in the village. She had always planned to go home for a visit, but she took ill and died in 1962.

Not all war brides made it to New Brunswick. Ada Cloke of Dover, Kent, met Murdoch Grant of Evandale, Kings County, and they were married early in 1918. According to news reports, Murdoch was "wounded three times and gassed once" during the course of his service. He wrote to his family on October 27, 1918, saying he was "in best of health and spirits," convalescing from his wounds. Tragically, he died in the flu epidemic at Bramshott camp in southern England a few days later. Ada and Murdoch had been married only nine months. His bride took his body to her home in Kent for burial. The inscription on his gravestone reads: "To my husband Murdoch Robey Grant, aged 24 of New Brunswick, Canada, died on Active Service 7.11.18."

A few war brides returned to their homelands after the breakup of their marriage or the death of a spouse, but the vast majority stayed in New Brunswick, where they raised families and helped build the province. Little did they know that, a quarter-century later, they would be on hand to welcome a new generation of war brides arriving in Canada after the Second World War.

Selected Bibliography

War Brides of the Second World War

Aikens, Gwladys M. Rees. *Nurses in Battledress: The World War II Story of a Member of the Q.A. Reserves*. Halifax, NS: Cymru Press, 1998.

Barrett, Barbara B., Eileen Dicks, Isobel Brown, Hilda Chaulk Murray, and Helen Fogwill Porter, eds. *We Came from Over the Sea: British War Brides in Newfoundland*. Portugal Cove, NL: British War Brides Association of Newfoundland and E.S. Press, 1996.

Broadfoot, Barry. *Six War Years 1939-1945: Memories of Canadians at Home and Abroad*. Toronto: PaperJacks, 1979.

Campbell, Gray. *We Found Peace*. Toronto: Thomas Allen, 1953.

Clapton, Eric. *Clapton: An Autobiography*. New York: Broadway Books, 2007.

Clark, Marilyn, and Courtney Clark. *War Brides: Our Sentimental Journey*. Regina, SK: Self-published, 2005.

Duivenvoorden-Mitic, Trudy, and J.P. LeBlanc. *Pier 21: The Gateway that Changed Canada*. Hantsport, NS: Lancelot Press, 1998.

Faryon, Cynthia J. *A War Bride's Story: Risking It All for Love After World War II*. Canmore, AB: Altitude Publishing Canada, 2004.

Granfield, Linda. *Brass Buttons and Silver Horseshoes: Stories from Canada's British War Brides*. Toronto: McClelland & Stewart, 2002.

Hibbert, Joyce, ed. *The War Brides*. Toronto: Peter Martin Associates, 1978.

Hickey, Rev. Father James Myles. *The Scarlet Dawn*. Campbellton, NB: Tribune Publishers, 1949.

Jarratt, Melynda. "The War Brides of New Brunswick." Master's thesis, University of New Brunswick, Fredericton, 1995.

———. *War Brides: The Stories of the Women Who Left Everything Behind to Follow the Men They Loved*. UK: Tempus Publishing, 2007.

Kozar, Judith. *Canada's War Grooms and the Girls Who Stole Their Hearts*. Renfrew, ON: General Store Publishing House, 2007.

Ladouceur, Barbara, and Phyllis Spence, eds. *Blackouts to Bright Lights: Canadian War Bride Stories*. Vancouver: Ronsdale Press, 1995.

Landry, Raymond. *En passant par les îles*. Saint Hubert, QC: Éditions REPER, 2003.

MacAuley, Peggy, and Horace R. MacAuley, eds. *Surrey Girl: Not Just Another War Bride*. rev. ed. Nepean, ON: HRM Publishing, 2006.

Maclay, Michael. *Aldershot's Canadians in Love and War 1939-45*. Farnborough, UK: Appin Publications, 1997.

McNeil, Bill. *Voices of a War Remembered: An Oral History of Canadians in World War Two*. Toronto: Doubleday Canada, 1992.

O'Hara, Peggy. *From Romance to Reality: Stories of Canadian War Brides*. Cobalt, ON: Highway Book Shop, Second printing, 1985.

O'Neill Dahm, Jacqueline. *The Last of the War Brides*. Canada: Trafford Publishing, n.d.

Rains, Olga, Lloyd Rains, and Melynda Jarratt. *Voices of the Left Behind: Project Roots and the Canadian War Children of World War Two*. Toronto: Dundurn Press, 2006.

Shewchuk, Helen. *If Kisses Were Roses: A 50th Anniversary Tribute to War Brides*. Sudbury, ON: Self-published, 1996.

Stacey, C.P., and Barbara M. Wilson. *The Half Million: The Canadians in Britain, 1939-1946*. Toronto: University of Toronto Press, 1987.

Walker, Joan. *Pardon My Parka*. Winnipeg, MB: Harlequin, 1958.

Wicks, Ben. *Promise You'll Take Care of My Daughter: The Remarkable War Brides of World War II*. Toronto: Stoddart, 1992.

War Brides of the First World War

Abraham, Dorothy. *Lone Cone: A Journal of Life on the West Coast of Vancouver Island*. 3rd ed. np: nd.

Gould, Florence E. "A War Bride Journey in 1917," *Okanagan History: The Thirty-seventh Report of the Okanagan Historical Society*, 1974.

Holmes, Peggy, and Joy Roberts. *It Could Have Been Worse*. Don Mills, ON: Collins, 1980.

Holmes, Peggy, and Andrea Spalding. *Never a Dull Moment*. Toronto: Collins, 1984.

Holmes, Peggy. *Still Soaring*. Edmonton, AB: Loon Books, 1987.

McKenna, M. Olga. *Micmac by Choice: Elsie Sark – An Island Legend*. Halifax, NS: Formac, 1990.

Morton, Desmond. *Fight or Pay: Soldiers' Families in the Great War*. Vancouver: University of British Columbia Press, 2004.

Strange, Kathleen. *With the West in Her Eyes: The Story of a Modern Pioneer*. Toronto: MacMillan Company of Canada, 1945.

Photo Credits

Photo on the front cover appears courtesy of Mary Oliver. The photos on pages 6 and 118 appear courtesy of Jean Belding. The photos on pages 8 and 91 appear courtesy of Alice Tranquilla. The photo on page 11 appears courtesy of Zoe Boone. The newspaper article on page 21 appears courtesy of *The Moncton Daily Times*. The photo on page 24 appears courtesy of Dorothy Hyslop. The photo on page 35 appears courtesy of the late Johan DeWitt. The photo on page 36 appears courtesy of Sandra Pond. The photo on page 39 appears courtesy of Angela Michaud. The photo on page 42 appears courtesy of Rita Maunder. The letter on page 44 appears courtesy of Russell Weller. The letter on page 45 appears courtesy of Rose Boulay. The photo on page 50 appears courtesy of Susan Willis. The photo on page 51 appears courtesy of Iona Loosen. The telegram on page 60 appears courtesy of Madeline Fitzgerald. The photo on page 64 appears courtesy of Jeannine Rasmussen. The photo on page 73 appears courtesy of Barbara Priestly. The photo on page 76 appears courtesy of Betty Hillman. The photo on page 79 appears courtesy of Hilda Jenkins Jarvis. The photo on page 80 appears courtesy of Dot Matchett. The letters on page 86 and 116 appear courtesy of Rose Burke. The photo on page 93 appears courtesy of Anna and Aurele Lavigne. The passport on page 95 appears courtesy of Deby Nash. The photo on page 101 appears courtesy of Lucy Jarratt. The documents on pages 102 and 104 appear courtesy of Library and Archives Canada (LAC). The newspaper article on page 110 appears courtesy of the *Telegraph-Journal*. The photo on page 112 appears courtesy of Gordon Hovey. The photo on page 119 appears courtesy of Doris Lloyd. The photo on page 126 appears courtesy of Rhoda Carrier. The wedding photo on the back cover appears courtesy of Cathie Elliot. The wedding certificate on the back cover appears courtesy of Vera Ruff. The map on page 16 is by Mike Bechthold. All illustrative material is reproduced by permission.

Index

A

Aberdeen Royal Mental Hospital 103
Aberdeen Scotland 27, 41, 56
Aldershot England 25, 27, 56, 57
American Revolutionary War 97
Amersfoort Holland 84, 85
Amos, Doris (Legate) 74
Amsterdam Holland 84, 85
Anderson, Isabella (Brand) 67-69
Anderson, Weldon 67, 68
Anfield NB 65
Antwerp Belgium 90, 91
Aquitania 8, 15, 16, 40, 42, 91, 107
Arthurette NB 38-40
Ashford England 129
Athabascan 36, 61
Athabascan II 61
Atholville NB 59
Avellino Italy 13, 92, 94
Ayr Scotland 38

B

Baden Austria 96
Baie du Vin NB 74
Baltic 129
Barr Hill Scotland 61
Bartibogue Bridge NB 67
Basie, Count 13
Bathurst NB 17, 49, 52, 53, 67, 89, 92, 93, 94, 100, 101, 110, 119
Bathurst Pulp and Paper 100

battles
  Battle of Britain 28, 31, 65, 96
  Battle of the Ardennes 8, 91
  Battle of the Bulge 90
  D-Day 48, 59, 92
  Gallipoli 29
Beatles 112, 113
Beattie, Marion (Robb) 50
Beaver Clubs 28
Belding, Jean (Attwood) 6, 29-30, 34
Belding, Jim 6
Belgium 11, 12, 13, 17, 83, 90, 91, 92, 129
Belledune NB 45, 46
Beny-sur-Mer Canadian War Cemetery 59
Bergen op Zoom Holland 79
Bermuda 11, 99
Black Loyalists 95, 97
Blanchette, Edna (Darby) 70, 71, 81
Blanchette, Tom 70
Bookham England 37
Boone, Marshall 56
Boone, Zoe (Blair) 11, 56, 57
Borgholm 100
Boston MA 75
Boulay, Horace 43, 45
Boulay, Rose (O'Reilly) 43, 45, 46
Bournemouth England 38
Boyd, Pattie 112, 113
Boy Scouts 119
Brighton England 60

Brighton train station 42
Bristol England 128
BritainGreat Britain 114
British Air Force 61
    Women's Auxiliary Air Force 30, 31, 32
British Army
    Auxiliary Territorial Service 30, 31, 32, 52, 56, 57, 66, 96
    Bicycle Corps 29
    Dental Corps 32
    Royal Observer Corps 72
    Women's Land Army 31, 33, 34, 35
British Auxiliary Fire Services 30
British Civil Defense
    Air Raid Precautions 30
    Women's Voluntary Services 30
British Commonwealth Air Training Plan 100
British National Fire Services 30, 38
British Navy
    Women's Royal Naval Service 30, 31, 33, 56
Brittain, Bill 38
Brock, Gloria 119
Brockway, May (Armstrong) 29
Brooks, Colonel A.J. 105
Brothers Two 113
Browne, Major-General B.W. 20
Brussels Belgium 49
Burke, Rose (Smith) 85
Burke, T.J. 55
Burnt Land Brook NB 78, 79
Burris, Maria Zellie (Despontin) 129
Burris, William 129
Burton NB 33, 35
Buzzel, Joyce (Ward) 28
Buzzel, Sergeant Ward 29

C

Camberwell England 128
Campbell, Betty (Sheppee) 38, 39, 40
Campbell, Howard 38
Campbellton NB 17, 129
Canadian Army 14, 15, 114
Canadian Army, Armoured Units
    8th Princess Louise's (New Brunswick) Hussars 25, 87, 92
Canadian Army, Artillery Units
    2nd Field Regiment 46, 110
    3rd Anti-Tank Regiment 67
    3rd Field Regiment 25
    5th Field Regiment 29
    6th Field Regiment 44
    8th Battery 92
    23rd Field Regiment 85
    90th Battery 25, 92
    104th Anti-Tank Battery 74
Canadian Army, Battalions
    55th Battalion 129
Canadian Army, Brigades
    3rd Infantry Brigade 25
Canadian Army, Divisions
    1st Infantry Division 17, 25
    3rd Infantry Division 17, 25
    5th Armoured Division 79
Canadian Army, Forestry Corps 67, 91, 103
Canadian Army, Infantry Units
    The Argyll and Sutherland Highlanders of Canada 79
    The Cameron Highlanders of Ottawa 70
    The Carleton and York Regiment 17, 25, 33, 35, 37, 41, 47, 53, 54, 55, 56, 65, 69, 92
    The New Brunswick Rangers 25
    The North Shore (New Brunswick) Regiment 17, 25, 43, 46, 52, 77, 89, 92

The Regina Rifle Regiment 113
The Royal Rifles of Canada 99
The Stormont, Dundas and
 Glengarry Highlanders 59, 60
Canadian Army, Provost Corps 75
Canadian Military Headquarters 48
Canadian National Railway 88
Canadian War Museum 72
Canadian Wives Bureau 15, 40-42, 48, 49, 50, 53, 56, 89, 92, 102-107
 Civilian Repatriation Section 48
 Information and Welfare Section 48
Carmania 129
Carson, James 126
Carson, Maud (Cornish) 126, 128
Carson, William 126, 128
Caterham England 36, 37, 55
Chaleur Bay 56, 77
Chartersville NB 87, 88
Chatham NB 67, 100
Cheshunt England 128
Chester England 57
Chestnut Canoe Factory 98
Chipman NB 65
Chunn, Charlie 59, 60
Clapp, Rose 112
Clapton, Eric 111-113
Clydebank Scotland 29
Concert Party 75
Cornhill NB 37
Corps of Commissionaires 74
Couillet Belgium 90, 91
Coulsdon England 54
Cranford England 6
Cricklewood England 45
Crimean War 27
Croydon Canucks War Brides Club 49, 50
Czechoslovkia 65

D

Daily Gleaner 117
Dalhousie NB 55, 56, 119, 129
Department of Mines and Resources
 Immigration Branch 14, 19, 22, 48, 84, 103, 104, 105
Department of National Defence 14, 19, 48, 106
Department of Veterans Affairs 14, 19, 20, 21, 22, 23, 58, 62, 65, 72, 73, 106, 109
Depression 17, 77, 81
DeWitt, Johan (Hillis) 33, 35
DeWitt, Private Luke 33, 35
Dickson, George "Bud" 59
Dickson, Merle 60
Dickson, Sylvia (Rusbridge) 59, 60
Dickson, Wallace 60
Dieppe NB 87
Distinguished Flying Cross 61
Doaktown NB 72, 74
Doorn Holland 9, 84, 85
Dorset England 32
Dorsey, Tommy 13, 37
Douglass, Kay 15
Douglastown NB 74
Dover England 130
Duncelt Scotland 103
Dunira Estate 33, 35
Dunkirk France 31, 100
Dunphy, Mabel (Cackett) 129
Dunphy, Peter 129

E

Eastbourne England 28
East Sussex 44
Edinburgh Scotland 27
Edinburgh War Brides Club 49, 51
Edmundston NB 22
Eel River Bar NB 55

Eel River Crossing NB 129
Eel River NB 119
Eindhoven Holland 87, 89
Elliot, Catherine (Robertson) 4, 41
Elliot, Glen 4
Elliot, Sergeant Glen 41
Emergency Powers (Defence) Act 30
Empire Brent 97
England 10, 25, 26, 32, 35, 37, 50, 52, 54, 56, 57, 59, 61, 65, 74, 75, 77, 78, 96, 108, 109, 110, 111, 112, 120, 129, 130
English Channel 12, 36, 48, 61
Evandale NB 130
Exmoor England 128

F

Fairfield NB 20
Ferris, Elva 50
Field, Mrs. 31
First World War 18, 29, 30, 65, 119, 127
Fitzgerald, James "Dewey" 60
Fitzgerald, Madeline (Rusbridge) Chunn 59, 60
Fledgling 11
France 13, 17, 26, 32, 47, 59, 91, 92, 129
Fredericton NB 10, 17, 22, 26, 28, 29, 31, 32, 51, 55, 60, 61, 62, 66, 70, 72, 91, 92, 95, 98, 99, 117, 120
Fredericton Singing War Brides 81
French Resistance 32
From Grief to Grace 66
Fryer, Edward 112
Fulham England 32
Fyffe, Hilda (Smith) 37
Fyffe, Sam 37

G

German Army 89
Germany 17, 28, 60, 88
Girdwood, Reverend 57

Girl Guides 119
Glasgow Scotland 29, 33, 34, 36, 43, 61
Glenlivet NB 70
Glen Tanar Scotland 67
Globe and Mail, The 20
Gourlay, Ron 113, 114
Grand Falls NB 35, 36
Grand Lake 97
Grand Manan Island NB 26
Grant, Ada (Cloke) 130
Grant, Annie (Hill) 66
Grant, Gunner David 67
Grant, Murdoch 130
Great Britain 11, 12, 13, 14, 15, 17, 19, 22, 25, 26, 27, 28, 29, 32, 37, 38, 42, 43, 46, 50, 54, 59, 61, 64, 65, 80, 81, 82, 91, 95, 96, 97, 98, 104, 109, 110
Greenock Scotland 25
Gregg, Milton F. 72, 73
Grover, Harold 60-61
Grover, Haroldene 61
Grover, Phyllis (Head) 60-61

H

Hacker, Irma 96, 97, 98, 99
Hague, Holland, The 49, 89
Halifax England 31
Halifax Explosion 127
Halifax Memorial 61
Halifax NS 10, 15, 26, 39, 40, 50, 52, 61, 85, 107, 111, 128, 129
Hamburg Germany 88
Hardwood Ridge NB 65
Harrington, Rifleman William 113, 114
Harrington, Winnifred (Gashen) 113, 114
Harrison, George 112
Hartland NB 33
Hawkins Corner NB 75
Hayden Ridge NB 113

Head, Phyllis Rose 44
Hennessy, Eileen 101
Hennessy, Lucy 100, 101
Hess, Rudolf 34, 36
Hibbert, Joyce 119
Hickey, Father Myles 43, 45, 46
Hickie, Annie (Gooseney) 99, 100
Hickie, Bill 99
Hillman, Betty (Lowthian) 75-76
Hillman, Doug 75-76
Hitler, Adolf 34, 36
Holborn England 34
Holder, Marjory 15
Holland 11, 12, 13, 14, 17, 83, 84, 85, 89, 90, 92, 109
Holmes, Barbara (Miles) 57-58
Holmes, Norman 57-58
Holten Holland 61
Holtville NB 126, 128
Home and School Association 119
Hong Kong 99
Hook of Holland 89
Hounslow England 29, 35
House of Commons 105
Huard, Barbara (Andrews) 119
Humber River 100
Hunter, Valreia 53
Hutchinson, Anne (Freestone) 50
Hyslop, Dorothy (Currie) 24, 119
Hyslop, Robert 24

I

Île de France 14
Îles de la Madeleine 17
Imhoff, Margaret 53
Imhoff, Mary (Didlick) 52-53
Imhoff, Regis 52-53
Imperial Order of Daughters of the Empire (IODE) 116-117
Indian Act 55
Ireland 11, 26, 43, 46

Islington England 46
Italy 11, 12, 13, 17, 69, 84, 92, 109

J

Jacquet River NB 46, 99
Japan 99
Jarvis, Hilda (Jones) Jenkins 78-79
Jenkins, Elaine 78-79
Jenkins, Hal 79
Jewish Aid Committee 96
John Deere Tractors 75
Johnston, Jack 36, 61, 62
Jones, George 108, 109
Juniper NB 113, 114

K

Kater, Albert 84, 87
Kater, Hetty 84, 87
Keegan, Pat 54
Keirstead, Winnifred (Green) 63, 65-66
Kenley England 31
Kilburn NB 67
Kilmarnock Scotland 38
Korea 64

L

Lac Baker NB 22
Lady Rodney 89, 91, 94
Lakeville Corner NB 94, 97, 98
Latteur, Adolphine 91
Lavigne, Anna (Perugine) 13, 92-94
Lavigne, Sergeant Aurele 13, 92-94
Lawrence, Ralph 34, 36, 61, 62
LeBlanc, Arsene 46, 47
LeBlanc, Edgar 47
LeBlanc, Elizabeth (van Gervan) 87, 88
LeBlanc, Trooper Ernest 87
LeBlanc, Sapper J.A. 92
LeBlanc, Joan (Hawtin) 46, 47

LeBlanc, Suzanne 92
Leeds England 72
Leicester England 56
Leigh England 66
Leipzig Germany 88
Letitia 75
Lewes England 44, 60
Lewisville NB 92
Liège Belgium 90
Liverpool England 15, 49, 89, 127
Lloyd, Anne 14
Lloyd, Doris (Field) 14, 31, 37, 120
Lloyd, Sergeant Ralph 37
London England 15, 27, 28, 31, 34, 42, 43, 49, 52, 63, 89, 96, 97, 113
Loosen, Mona (Ogg) 49, 51
Loosen, Flying Officer Philip 49
Losier, Dr. Percy 68
Lower Glencoe NS 112
Ludlow MA 75

M

MacDonald, Brian 112, 113
MacDonald, Cheryl 112
MacDonald, Frank 112, 113
MacDonald, Heather 112, 113
MacDonald, Patricia (Clapton) 112
Mackellar, Leading Aircraftsman Jack 38
MacKellar, Mary (Ralston) 38
MacKinnon, Catherine (Baker) 105
Maillet, Flavien 69
Maillet, Yvonne (French) 69, 70
Marche-les-dames Belgium 129
Marks, Doris (Farrow) 77, 78
Marney, Alden 129
Marney, Ethel Violet (Mitchell) 127, 129
Marney, Glenn 129
Marney, William 127, 129

Massey, Alice (Parkin) 28
Massey, Vincent 28
Matchett, Blair 56, 57, 80
Matchett, Dot (Upton) 56, 57, 80
Matchett, Edith (Upton) 10
Maugerville NB 16
Maunder, Rita (Scrase) 42
Mauretania 15, 49, 53
McAdam NB 17, 53
McArthur, Brenda (Rudd) 53
McArthur, Ivan 53
McArthur, Robert 53
McKnight, A. (Kennedy) 118
McLenaghan, Maureen 74
McLenaghan, Norman 74
McLenaghan, Rose (Connoly) 74
Mearnskirk Scotland 61
Merry Tadpole 27, 110
Mesheau, Bill 75
Mesheau, Eileen (Meaden) 32, 75
Metagama 129
Military Cross 109
Miller, Glenn 13, 37
Millmeece England 11
Millville NB 8, 9, 75, 91, 92
Minto NB 65, 66
Miramichi Irish Festival 74
Miramichi NB 17, 57, 67, 69, 74
Miscou Island NB 26, 77, 78
Moncton NB 15, 16, 17, 22, 26, 46, 50, 52, 58, 69, 75, 87, 92, 99
Mons University 90
Montcalm 129
Montreal QC 26, 98, 112
Mostyn Hostel 15
Mount Allison University 18
Mullin, Kate (Smith) 128, 129
Mullin, Private Samuel 128
Murray, Eileen (Goulding) 74
Murray, Mae (Goulding) 74
Murray, Willard 110, 111

N

Nadeau, Elsie (Spinner) 119
Naples Italy 13, 93, 94
Nash, Amy 97
Nash, Deby 98
Nash, Denise 98
Nash, Diane 97, 98
Nash, Dorrit (Hacker) 94, 95, 96, 97, 98, 99
Nash, Hedley 95, 97, 98
Nashwaaksis NB 34, 36, 61, 62
Nassau Bahamas 98
National Service Act 30
Navy, Army and Air Force Institutes (NAAFI) 31
Netherlands. *See* Holland
New Brunswick Legislature 55
New Brunswick Telephone Company 129
New Brunswick War Brides Association (NBWBA) 120
Newcastle NB 67, 80
Newfoundland 11, 99
Newport England 75
Newport Wales 57
Niagara Falls ON 74
Normandy France 13, 32, 59, 60, 92
Northland 127
Norway 100, 101
Norwegian merchant navy 100, 101
Nuremburg Trials 34

O

O'Brien, Mary 43
Operation Daddy 49
Oromocto NB 112, 113
Oslo Norway 100
Ottawa ON 75
Ouellette, Jean-Marie "John" 88, 89
Ouellette, Maria (Egbars) 88, 89, 94

P

Paine, Sandra (Wariner) 110, 111
Palestine 96
Palmater, Frank 55
Palmater, Mary (Parr) 55, 56
Palmater, Sheila 55
Paris France 49
Paul, Charlie 54, 55
Paul, Christine 54
Paul, Cindy 54
Paul, Jean (Keegan) 53, 54, 55
Paul, Jim 54
Perth-Andover NB 54, 67, 77
Peterborough ON 59
Peters, Gloria (Hassel) 99
Pier 21 10, 40, 52
Pinder NB 129
Plaster Rock NB 10, 14, 35, 65, 78, 119, 120
Plume, Christina 128
Plymouth England 38, 40
Polegate England 110
Portland Dockyards 32
Preston England 38

Q

Queen Elizabeth 58
Queen Mary 15, 40, 52, 53
Quinn, Ed 68
Quinn, Mrs. 68
Quispamsis NB 100

R

Rasmussen, Jeannine 65
Ravenstein Holland 89
Red Bank NB 57
Red Cross 14, 15, 20, 28, 34, 50, 53, 54, 64, 77, 88, 105, 106, 117, 118
  Training Meeting Committee 53
  Welfare Committee 54

Redhill England 57
Redmondville NB 67
Reigate England 57
Renfrewshire Scotland 34
Richibucto NB 67
Ringmer England 69
Rioux, Ivan 35
Rioux, Nancy (King) 10, 35
Ripley England 111
Roffey England 77
Rogersville NB 69, 70
Rowena NB 56
Royal Australian Air Force 100
Royal Canadian Air Force 58, 72
Royal Canadian Legion 27, 109, 111, 117, 119
Royal Ordnance Factory 46
Ruddick, Kay (Douglass) 50, 52
Ruff, Vera (Dauncey) 119
Rutledge, Floyd 72, 73, 74
Rutledge, Winifred (Martin) 72, 73, 74

S

Sackville House 49
Sackville NB 17
St. Agnes Catholic Church 45
St. Andrews NB 58
St. Augustine's Church 38
St. Catharines ON 74
St. Croix IODE 116, 117
St. Dunstan's Church 6
Saint John NB 17, 26, 28, 50, 52, 58, 71, 79, 85, 99, 109, 117, 127, 128, 129
Saint John's NL 99
St. John River 16
Saint John Temperance Society 118
St. John the Evangelist Church 46, 47
St. Louis-de-Kent NB 70
St. Margaret's NB 67
Saint Paul NB 99

St. Stephen NB 22, 24, 38, 58, 59, 70, 85, 87, 119
Salisbury England 32
Salisbury NB 75
Salvation Army 28
Samaria 112
Saskatchewan War Brides Association (SWBA) 120
Scandinavian 128
Scarlet Dawn, The 43
Scotland 11, 26, 27, 33, 35, 67, 102, 103, 113, 114
Scythia 40
Second World War 12, 13, 25, 28, 30, 34, 37, 41, 81, 93, 100, 108, 121, 126, 130
Shaw, Artie 13
Sheffield NB 47
Shippegan NB 94
Shoreham-by-Sea England 70
Sicily Italy 17, 56
Siddon Ridge NB 41
Sillikers NB 10, 26, 57, 80
Slough England 79
Smith, Betty (Silk) 38
Smith, Seldon 38
Smith, Selma (Kater) 9, 84, 85, 86, 87, 116, 117
Smith, Sidney 9, 85, 86, 87
SMT Eastern 75
Southampton England 15, 91, 107
Sowers, Sergeant Major Harold 16, 47, 48
Sowers, Mildred (Young) 16, 47
Spanish Point Bermuda 99
Summerside PE 112, 113
Sussex NB 37, 79, 118
Swynnerton England 46
Sydney Australia 100

T

Tabusintac NB 110, 111
Telegraph-Journal 20, 48, 50, 71, 100, 110, 117
Thomas, Mrs. 58
Thornton Heath England 47
Thurnheer, Alice 98
Tide Head NB 59
Titus, I.K. 118
Titus, Mrs. I.K. 118
Tobique Indian Reserve NB 56
Tobique NB 54
Tompkins, Earlin 65
Tompkins, Edith (Dasch) 64, 65
Toppin, Quentin Douglas 100
Toppin, Ruth (Harris) 100
Tranquilla, Augustine "Alice" (Rondeau) 8, 9, 90, 91
Tranquilla, Jim 8, 90, 91
Trans-Canada Airlines 57
Trocadero 97
Tunisian 128
Twickenham England 53

U

Union of New Brunswick Indians 55
United States 20, 75
University of Naples 92
University of New Brunswick 18, 62, 72, 73
Upper Kintore NB 77
Upper Mills NB 9, 22, 85, 87, 117
Urmston England 105
Utrecht Holland 84, 89
Uxbridge England 31

V

Van Der Mude, Mardy (Holder) 50
Veterans Land Act 18
Vienna Austria 94, 96, 97
Volunteer Aid Detachments 28

W

W.H. Smith & Sons 34
Waddlow, Jerry 66
Wales 11, 26, 57, 59
War Brides, The 119
Ward, William 29
Wariner, Marjorie 110, 111
Wariner, Willard 110
Waweig NB 58
Weller, Russel 60, 61
Wesenberg, Anna (Hennessy) 100, 101
Wesenberg, Captain Henrik 100, 101
Weymouth England 32
White, Bill 107, 108
White, Colleen 107, 108
White, Sally 107, 108
Wilby, Delice (deWolf) 10, 31, 32
Wilby, Gunner Thomas 31, 32
Willingdon England 67
Withers, Kathleen (Smith) 20
Women's Institute 117
Woodstock NB 25, 65, 105, 129
Worthing England 59

Y

Year of the War Bride 55, 120
York England 32
Young Men's Christian Association (YMCA) 27, 35, 117, 118
Young Women's Christian Association (YWCA) 128

The New Brunswick Military Heritage Project

The New Brunswick Military Heritage Project, a non-profit organization devoted to public awareness of the remarkable military heritage of the province, is an initiative of the Brigadier Milton F. Gregg, VC, Centre for the Study of War and Society of the University of New Brunswick. The organization consists of museum professionals, teachers, university professors, graduate students, active and retired members of the Canadian Forces, and other historians. We welcome public involvement. People who have ideas for books or information for our database can contact us through our Web site: www.unb.ca/nbmhp.

One of the main activities of the New Brunswick Military Heritage Project is the publication of the New Brunswick Military Heritage Series with Goose Lane Editions. This series of books is under the direction of Marc Milner, Director of the Gregg Centre, and J. Brent Wilson, Publications Director of the Gregg Centre at the University of New Brunswick. Publication of the series is supported by a grant from the Canadian War Museum.

The New Brunswick Military Heritage Series

Volume 1
Saint John Fortifications, 1630-1956, Roger Sarty and Doug Knight

Volume 2
Hope Restored: The American Revolution and the Founding of New Brunswick, Robert L. Dallison

Volume 3
The Siege of Fort Beauséjour, 1755, Chris M. Hand

Volume 4
Riding into War: The Memoir of a Horse Transport Driver, 1916-1919, James Robert Johnston

Volume 5
The Road to Canada: The Grand Communications Route from Saint John to Quebec, W. E. (Gary) Campbell

Volume 6
Trimming Yankee Sails: Pirates and Privateers of New Brunswick, Faye Kert

Volume 7
War on the Home Front: The Farm Diaries of Daniel MacMillan, 1914-1927, ed. Bill Parenteau and Stephen Dutcher

Volume 8

Turning Back the Fenians: New Brunswick's Last Colonial Campaign,
Robert L. Dallison

Volume 9

*D-Day to Carpiquet: The North Shore Regiment and
the Liberation of Europe,* Marc Milner

Volume 10

Hurricane Pilot: The Wartime Letters of Harry F. Gill, DFM, 1940-1943,
ed. Brent Wilson with Barbara J. Gill

Volume 11

*The Bitter Harvest of War: New Brunswick and
the Conscription Crisis of 1917,* Andrew Theobald

About the Author

Melynda Jarratt is the leading authority on the history of the Canadian war brides of the Second World War. Originally from Bathurst, Melynda has a Bachelor of Arts (Honours) and a Master of Arts in History from the University of New Brunswick in Fredericton. She wrote her Master's thesis on the New Brunswick war brides of the Second World War and has continued to document their story for more than twenty years. Melynda also has a diploma in Digital Media and Design and runs her own information technology company in Fredericton, specializing in heritage, arts, and culture, as well as the website, www.CanadianWarBrides.com.

Melynda has worked as a consultant for the Queen Mary II History of Cunard Exhibition, Statistics Canada Portraits of Canada, the Department of Veterans Affairs, and Canada Post, and has appeared as a subject matter expert in television and radio documentaries. She is the co-author of *Voices of the Left Behind* (Dundurn, 2006) and *War Brides: The Stories of the Women Who Left Everything Behind to Follow the Men They Loved* (Tempus, 2007). Melynda was the driving force behind the Year of the War Bride in 2006 and organized the 60th anniversary launch at Pier 21 on February 9, 2006. She also curated an exhibition on New Brunswick war brides at the York Sunbury Museum in Fredericton, and has appeared several times before parliamentary committees as an expert witness on war bride citizenship. She played a leading role in the passage of the "Lost Canadians" Bill C-37 in April 2008.

Melynda Jarratt lives in Fredericton with her husband, Dan Weston.